ZAGAT®

Vancouver

2010

Including Victoria, Vancouver Island
& Whistler

LOCAL EDITORS
Tim Pawsey with Heather Pawsey
STAFF EDITOR
Cynthia Kilian

Published and distributed by
Zagat Survey, LLC
4 Columbus Circle
New York, NY 10019
T: 212.977.6000
E: vancouver@zagat.com
www.zagat.com

ACKNOWLEDGMENTS

We thank Gary Hynes, Shelora Sheldon and Steven Shukow, as well as
the following members of our staff: Stacey Slate (editorial assistant),
Brian Albert, Sean Beachell, Maryanne Bertollo, Jane Chang, Sandy
Cheng, Reni Chin, Larry Cohn, Alison Flick, Jeff Freier, Roy Jacob,
Natalie Lebert, Mike Liao, Andre Pilette, Becky Ruthenburg, Sharon
Yates, Anna Zappia and Kyle Zolner.

© 2009 Zagat Survey, LLC
ISBN-13: 978-1-60478-153-3
ISBN-10: 1-60478-153-x
Printed in the
United States of America

Contents

About This Survey

Here are the results of our **2010 Vancouver Restaurants Survey,** covering 298 of the city's finest restaurants, nightspots and attractions. Like all our guides, this one is based on input from avid local consumers – 2,721 all told. We've also added a selection of top-rated hotels.

OUR PHILOSOPHY: Three premises underlie our ratings and reviews. First, we believe that the collective opinions of large numbers of knowledgeable consumers are more accurate than the opinion of one critic. Second, there are many parts of the equation when choosing a restaurant, nightspot, hotel or attraction, thus we ask surveyors to rate each aspect separately. Finally, since people need reliable information in a fast, easy-to-digest format, we strive to be concise and to provide plenty of handy indexes and Top Lists.

JOIN IN: To improve this guide or any aspect of our performance, we solicit your comments. Just contact us at **nina-tim@zagat.com.** We also invite you to join our surveys yearlong at **ZAGAT.com.** Do so and you'll receive a choice of rewards in exchange.

Z **ABOUT ZAGAT:** In 1979, we started asking friends to rate and review restaurants purely for fun. That hobby grew into Zagat Survey; 31 years later, we have over 350,000 surveyors and cover everything from airlines to shopping. Along the way, we evolved from being a publisher of print guides to a provider of digital content in a full range of formats: **ZAGAT.com, ZAGAT.mobi** (for web-enabled mobile devices), **ZAGAT TO GO** (for smartphones) and **nru** (for Android phones). We also produce customized content for numerous corporate custom clients.

THANKS: We're grateful to our local editors, Tim Pawsey, food and wine journalist and contributor to numerous publications; and Heather Pawsey, a professional opera singer with a journalistic background and a passion for gastronomy. We also sincerely thank the thousands of surveyors who participated – all of our content is really "theirs."

New York, NY
November 30, 2009

Nina and Tim

Nina and Tim Zagat

What's New

The excitement surrounding the 2010 Winter Olympics and Paralympics has helped keep Vancouver on top of its culinary game despite the global economic slowdown. The city welcomed an eclectic buffet of newcomers, including hotly anticipated arrivals from superstar French-American chefs Daniel Boulud (at **db Bistro Moderne** and a re-vitalized **Lumière** on the West Side) and Jean-Georges Vongerichten (at **Market by Jean-Georges** Downtown). And the financial tumult had some upsides for surveyors, with 40% reporting better deals and 33% feeling their patronage is more appreciated.

DOWNTOWN UPSTARTS: Downtown's dining boom contin-ues. Japanese seafooder **Miku** adds *aburi* (grilled sushi) to the mix, **Voya** injects Eclectic flair into the Loden Hotel and Italian **Cibo Trattoria** wows with sommelier Sebastien Le Goff. Granville Street greeted Eclectic hot spots **The Edge** and **The Refinery,** the latter's eco-conscious ethos speaking to the 81% of surveyors for whom eating "green" is important.

WEST SIDE STORY: West Side arrivals should please the 24% of surveyors who are frequenting less-costly places since the economy's slide. Chef Angus An shuttered his upscale **Gastropod** to reopen it as the more casual Thai **Maenam**, while **Trattoria Italian Kitchen** debuted as a lower-priced sibling of Downtown's **Italian Kitchen.**

FRINGE BENEFITS: Newcomers have sprouted in unlikely East Side backwaters: fondue fans can find a fix at bistro **Au Petit Chavignol**; affordable French fare rules at **Les Faux Bourgeois**; and funky **2 Chefs & a Table** serves Pacific Northwest tasting plates almost on the docks. Gastown welcomed top bartender Jay Jones' **Pourhouse** and its Eclectic kitchen.

IN THE WINGS: At press time, chocolate lovers await the West Side's **Thomas Haas Patisserie,** and **Corner Suite Bistro De Luxe** is about to debut Downtown with chef Anthony Sedlak. Looking ahead, "Laird of Gastown" Sean Heather plans taparia **Judas Goat,** and Asian-influenced **Oru** will open at Downtown's Fairmont Pacific Rim hotel.

Vancouver   Tim Pawsey
November 30, 2009

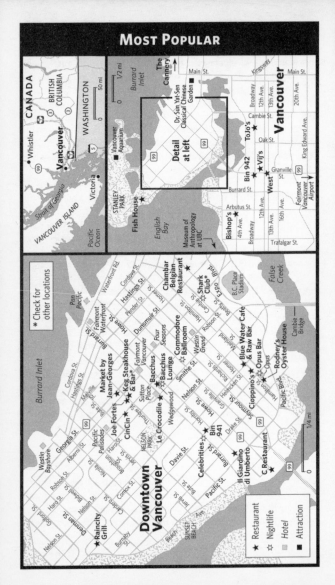

40,000 places to eat, drink, stay & play - free at ZAGAT.com

Most Popular

1. Vij's | *Indian*
2. Keg Steak | *Steak*
3. Blue Water Cafe | *Seafood*
4. Le Crocodile | *French*
5. Chambar | *Belgian*
6. C Restaurant | *Seafood*
7. Bishop's | *Pacific NW*
8. West | *Pacific NW*
9. ToJo's | *Japanese*
10. Joe Fortes | *Seafood/Steak*
11. Cannery | *Seafood*
12. Bin 941/942 | *Eclectic*
13. Raincity Grill | *Pacific NW*
14. Bacchus | *French*
15. Cioppino's | *Mediterranean*
16. Market by Jean-Georges | *French*
17. Fish House | *Seafood*
18. CinCin | *Italian*
19. Il Giardino | *Italian*
20. Rodney's Oyster | *Seafood*

It's obvious that many of the above restaurants are among Vancouver's most expensive, but if popularity were calibrated to price, we suspect that a number of other restaurants would join their ranks. Thus, we have added a list of Best Buys on page 11.

The map on the facing page includes Vancouver's Most Popular restaurants, nightspots and attractions, and some top hotels. See page 72 for a list of Most Popular nightlife venues, and page 80 for Most Popular attractions.

KEY NEWCOMERS

Our editors' take on the year's top restaurant arrivals.

Au Petit Chavignol | *French*

Cibo Trattoria | *Italian*

db Bistro Moderne | *French*

La Brasserie | *French/German*

Les Faux Bourgeois | *French*

Maenam | *Thai*

Market/Jean-Georges | *French*

Miku Restaurant | *Japanese*

Nook | *Italian*

Pourhouse | *Eclectic*

r.tl | *Eclectic*

Voya | *Eclectic*

Ratings & Symbols

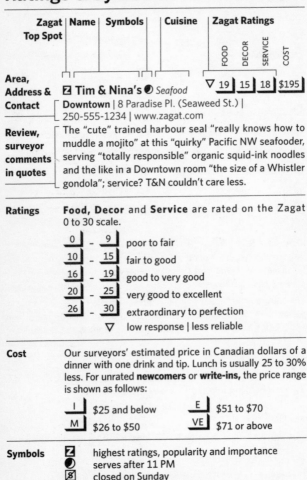

	Zagat Top Spot	Name	Symbols	Cuisine	Zagat Ratings

Area, Address & Contact

☑ Tim & Nina's ◑ *Seafood* ▽ 19 | 15 | 18 | $195

Downtown | 8 Paradise Pl. (Seaweed St.) | 250-555-1234 | www.zagat.com

Review, surveyor comments in quotes

The "cute" trained harbour seal "really knows how to muddle a mojito" at this "quirky" Pacific NW seafooder, serving "totally responsible" organic squid-ink noodles and the like in a Downtown room "the size of a Whistler gondola"; service? T&N couldn't care less.

Ratings   **Food, Decor** and **Service** are rated on the Zagat 0 to 30 scale.

0 – 9	poor to fair
10 – 15	fair to good
16 – 19	good to very good
20 – 25	very good to excellent
26 – 30	extraordinary to perfection
▽	low response	less reliable

Cost   Our surveyors' estimated price in Canadian dollars of a dinner with one drink and tip. Lunch is usually 25 to 30% less. For unrated **newcomers** or **write-ins,** the price range is shown as follows:

I	$25 and below	**E**	$51 to $70
M	$26 to $50	**VE**	$71 or above

Symbols

☑	highest ratings, popularity and importance
◑	serves after 11 PM
⑤	closed on Sunday
Ⓜ	closed on Monday
⊅	no credit cards accepted

Top Food Ratings

Excludes places with low votes.

28 La Belle Auberge | *French*
Vij's | *Indian*
Cioppino's | *Mediterranean*

27 Le Crocodile | *French*
ToJo's | *Japanese*
Bishop's | *Pacific NW*
West | *Pacific NW*
Shiro Japanese | *Japanese*

26 Il Giardino | *Italian*
Blue Water Cafe | *Seafood*
Lumière | *French*
Vij's Rangoli | *Indian*
Kitanoya Guu | *Japanese*
Maenam | *Thai*
Market/Jean-Georges | *French*

La Régalade | *French*
Au Petit Chavignol | *French*
Fuel | *Pacific NW*
Kingyo | *Japanese*
La Buca | *Italian*
Chambar | *Belgian*
Diva at the Met | *Pacific NW*
L'Altro Buca | *Italian*

25 Pear Tree | *Continental*
La Quercia | *Italian*
La Terrazza | *Italian*
Bin 941/942 | *Eclectic*
C Restaurant | *Seafood*
Provence Med. | *French/Med.*
Q4 | *Italian*

BY CUISINE

CHINESE

25 Sun Sui Wah
Kirin Mandarin
24 Kirin Seafood
23 Imperial Chinese
Wild Rice

ECLECTIC

25 Bin 941/942
24 Cafe Medina
Trafalgar's Bistro
22 Voya
21 Nu

FRENCH

28 La Belle Auberge
27 Le Crocodile

26 Lumière
Market/Jean-Georges
La Régalade

ITALIAN

26 Il Giardino
La Buca
L'Altro Buca
25 La Quercia
La Terrazza

JAPANESE

27 ToJo's
Shiro Japanese
26 Kitanoya Guu
Kingyo
24 Gyoza King

PACIFIC NORTHWEST

27 Bishop's
West
26 Fuel
Diva at the Met
25 Cru

SEAFOOD

26 Blue Water Cafe
25 C Restaurant

Sun Sui Wah
Go Fish!
24 Rodney's Oyster

STEAKHOUSES

24 Gotham Steak
Hy's Encore
22 Joe Fortes
Kobe
20 Shore Club

Top Decor

26 Seasons In Park
Five Sails
Fraîche
25 Yew
Teahouse in Stanley Park
Lift
Il Giardino

La Terrazza*
Bacchus
Shore Club
Blue Water Cafe
Market/Jean-Georges
24 Watermark
West

Top Service

27 Bishop's
Le Crocodile
26 La Belle Auberge
West
Au Petit Chavignol
Mistral Bistro
Fleuri

La Terrazza
25 Il Giardino
Pear Tree
Vij's
Bacchus
Cioppino's
Fraîche

---

* Indicates a tie with restaurant above

Best Buys

In order of Bang for the Buck rating.

1. Nat's NY Pizzeria
2. Pajo's
3. Go Fish!
4. Vera's Burger
5. Tomahawk Barbecue
6. Cafe Medina
7. Saravanaa Bhavan
8. Nuba Restaurant/Café
9. Vij's Rangoli
10. Gyoza King

Victoria & Vancouver Island

MOST POPULAR

1. Keg Steak | *Steak*
2. Brasserie L'Ecole | *French*
3. Sooke Harbour | *Pacific NW*
4. Empress Room | *Pacific NW*
5. Zambri's | *Italian*

TOP FOOD

28	Panache	*Pacific NW*
27	Sobo	*Eclectic*
	Hastings Hse.	*Pacific NW*
	Sooke Harbour	*Pacific NW*
	Camille's	*Pacific NW*

TOP DECOR

28	Empress Room
27	Pointe/Wickaninnish
26	Panache
	Hastings Hse.
	Sooke Harbour

TOP SERVICE

28	Hastings Hse.
27	Panache
	Rest. Matisse
26	Camille's
	Brasserie L'Ecole

Whistler

MOST POPULAR

1. Keg Steak | *Steak*
2. Araxi | *Pacific NW*
3. Bear Foot Bistro | *Pacific NW*
4. Hy's Steak | *Steak*
5. Rim Rock | *Pacific NW/Seafood*

TOP FOOD

27	Bear Foot Bistro	*Pacific NW*
26	Rim Rock	*Pacific NW/Seafood*
	Araxi	*Pacific NW*
25	La Rua	*Pacific NW*
	Elements	*Eclectic*

TOP DECOR

24	Edgewater Lodge
23	Araxi
	Rim Rock
22	Il Caminetto
	Wildflower

TOP SERVICE

26	Bear Foot Bistro
25	Rim Rock
	Araxi
24	Il Caminetto
	Hy's Steak

40,000 places to eat, drink, stay & play – free at ZAGAT.com

DINING
DIRECTORY

	FOOD	DECOR	SERVICE	COST

Dining

Vancouver

Amarcord *Italian*   22 | 18 | 21 | $48
Yaletown | 104-1168 Hamilton St. (bet. Davie & Helmcken Sts.) |
604-681-6500 | www.amarcord.ca
Regulars of this Yaletown "old guard of Italian cuisine" hail the "best
gnocchi this side of Tuscany", "over-the-top lobster pasta" and other
"elegant", "dependable", "reasonably priced" fare delivered with
"warm", "unhurried" service; though some snipe it's "time for a face-
lift", others find the setting "homey but romantic" and the experience
"still lovely after all these years"; N.B. a new owner arrived post-Survey.

Aqua Riva *Pacific NW*   20 | 21 | 21 | $50
Downtown | 200 Granville St. (Cordova St.) | 604-683-5599 |
www.aquariva.com
"Watch the Seabus come in" while enjoying a "lovely view of the harbour" at this casual Downtown Pacific Northwester where "tasty fare",
"quick, reliable service" and an "attractive, contemporary" room draw
everyone from "suits for lunch" to "lots of tourists"; quibblers gripe it's
"a little overpriced", but fans counter "it's the setting that counts."

Z NEW Au Petit Chavignol *French*   26 | 22 | 26 | $41
East Side | 845 E. Hastings St. (bet. Campbell & Hawks Aves.) |
604-255-4218 | www.aupetitchavignol.com *Key Newcomer*
"Hello cheese heaven!" gush groupies of this "off-the-beaten-track"
East Side French bistro where the "inspired" offerings include "amazing charcuterie", "proper" fondues and raclette, all "expertly
matched" with "a magical wine list" and served by "intelligent" "people who care"; yes, the neighbourhood's "dodgy", but there's a "cosy
atmosphere" inside and the herd insists "everyone must eat here" – or
at least visit the adjacent shop, Les Amis du Fromage.

Bacchus *French*   25 | 25 | 25 | $66
Downtown | Wedgewood Hotel | 845 Hornby St. (bet. Robson & Smithe Sts.) |
604-608-5319 | www.wedgewoodhotel.com
The "beautiful staff" "does everything right" at this Downtown French
that's the "ultimate place to splurge" on chef Lee Parsons' "exquisitely

prepared and plated" fare presented in a "sumptuous" setting that's "as well-upholstered as its denizens" (including "movie stars"); while power brokers "get deals done" in the fireplace lounge, romantics retreat to the "classy, clubby" dining room with "shimmering candlelight" and "lovely piano music" for a "discreet rendezvous" or to "fall in love all over again."

Bacchus Bistro M *French* — 24 | 19 | 21 | $44

Langley | Domaine de Chaberton | 1064 216th St. (16th Ave.) | 604-530-9694 | www.domainedechaberton.com

Devotees drive to "the middle of nowhere" (Langley, actually) for the "superb" "seasonal" French fare at this bistro in a "country-style" setting at Domaine de Chaberton winery; "attentive service" and a "huge patio surrounded by vineyards" add to the "good value", but it's best "not to go without a phone call" first, as dinner is served Friday and Saturday only (lunch Wednesday–Sunday).

Beach House at Dundarave Pier *Pacific NW* — 22 | 23 | 21 | $59

West Vancouver | 150 25th St. (Bellevue Ave.) | 604-922-1414 | www.atthebeachhouse.com

The "magnificent" view of "Howe Sound and the Downtown city skyline" draws fin fans to this "romantic" Pacific Northwester situated "right down by the water in West Vancouver", where "lots of fresh seafood" is delivered by "relaxed but attentive" servers; though a few carp about the "hefty tab", a post-prandial "walk on the seawall" shores up the appeal.

#12

Bin 941 Tapas Parlour ◐ *Eclectic* — 25 | 19 | 21 | $42

West End | 941 Davie St. (bet. Burrard & Howe Sts.) | 604-683-1246

Bin 942 Tapas Parlour ◐ *Eclectic*

West Side | 1521 W. Broadway (bet. Fir & Granville Sts.) | 604-734-9421 www.bin941.com

All that's "small" "rules" at these "crazy busy" West End and West Side "tapas-size" siblings where chef Gord Martin's Eclectic "bites" deliver "robust" flavours; "friendly, informative service" and a "lively", "funky" vibe help make them a "real find, especially for late-night" noshers who don't mind "close quarters" and music so "earsplitting" "you can't hear yourself drink."

	FOOD	DECOR	SERVICE	COST

☑ Bishop's *Pacific NW*

| 27 | 23 | 27 | $77 |

West Side | 2183 W. Fourth Ave. (bet. Arbutus & Yew Sts.) | 604-738-2025 | www.bishopsonline.com

Diners "feel loved, not just well-fed" at John Bishop's Pacific Northwest "classic" on the West Side that again ranks No. 1 for Service in the Vancouver Survey, courtesy of the "charming, thoughtful host"-owner and his "gracious", "flawless" staff; the "local, organic movement" plays out in "exceptional cuisine" that's served in a "simple yet elegant room", adding up to a "consistently pure and classy", if "pricey", evening partisans praise as "impeccable in every sense."

Bistro Pastis Ⓜ *French*

| 24 | 21 | 23 | $54 |

West Side | 2153 W. Fourth Ave. (bet. Arbutus & Yew Sts.) | 604-731-5020 | www.pastis.ca

"Other bistros may be newer or hipper", but fans of John Blakeley's "unflaggingly French" West Side "neighbourhood favourite" swear by its "well-wrought classics" (including coq au vin) and its "sure hand with seafood", all served by a "knowledgeable" staff; the "inviting" setting conjures up a "side street in Paris" where "you always feel like a regular, even if you aren't."

Bistrot Bistro *French*

| 22 | 19 | 21 | $47 |

West Side | 1961 W. Fourth Ave. (bet. Cypress & Maple Sts.) | 604-732-0004 | www.bistrotbistro.com

It's a "delightful little piece of France in Kits" profess patrons of this West Side bistro "owned and run by a French couple" and specialising in "honest", "exemplary comfort food"; the "three-course Sunday–Thursday menu is a value" say fans, and an "unpretentious staff" and colourful setting with slate floors add to a scene that "radiates laid-back sophistication."

☑ Blue Water Cafe & Raw Bar ❶ *Seafood*

| 26 | 25 | 24 | $73 |

Yaletown | 1095 Hamilton St. (Helmcken St.) | 604-688-8078 | www.bluewatercafe.net

"In a city with a school of competition", fin fans hie to chef Frank Pabst's "posh" converted warehouse in Yaletown, where "flawless", "sumptuous seafood" is served in "innovative", "eye-popping presentations" by an "outstanding" staff; an "elegant" raw bar for sushi and "oysters that are pure bliss", plus "extensive wine" offerings help fuel a "bustling" "see-and-be-seen" scene – just be sure to "bring the expense-account card."

Boneta ⏺🆔 *French* | 24 | 22 | 23 | $57 |

Gastown | 1 Cordova St. W. (Carrall St.) | 604-684-1844 | www.boneta.ca

Diners who "like something different" "with a youthful twist" are drawn to this "hip", "edgy" "Gastown oasis" in a "bustling", "cool industrial" heritage room where chef Jeremie Bastien turns out an "excellent", "constantly evolving" "eclectic" French menu of "playful but serious" fare; "ultracreative cocktails", "amazing service" and "prices that are not too bad" complete a "full package" surveyors say is "just what the neighbourhood needed" – and "very Vancouver."

Brix ⏺🆔 *Pacific NW* | 21 | 23 | 20 | $57 |

Yaletown | 1138 Homer St. (bet. Davie & Helmcken Sts.) | 604-915-9463 | www.brixvancouver.com

It "feels like Europe" to surveyors "dining in the atrium" on the "lovely courtyard patio" at this "sturdy" Pacific Northwest "standby in trendy Yaletown"; the "historic building", some 60 wines by the glass and a 2 AM closing are additional draws, though a few fret over "uneven service"; N.B. the adjacent lounge, George, has a small, creative menu.

Café de Paris 🆔 *French* | 21 | 17 | 21 | $51 |

West End | 751 Denman St. (bet. Alberni & Robson Sts.) | 604-687-1418

For a "slice of Paris" in the West End, this long-running "simple but well-priced" "classic" French bistro "remains true to form and tradition"; though some sniff it's "nothing exciting" (including the decor), advocates appreciate the "understated" feel and some of the "best frites in town."

Cafe Il Nido 🆔 *Italian* | 20 | 18 | 21 | $51 |

Downtown | 780 Thurlow St. (Robson St.) | 604-685-6436 | www.cafeilnido.net

Located Downtown, this "cute" West End "hideaway" "whisks you back to Tuscany or wherever you left your heart in Italy" with its "reasonably priced" fare including "flavourful pastas"; if some find it "reliable if unexciting" with decor that's a bit "outdated", "master host" Franco Felice and his "gracious staff" plus a "pretty" "garden patio" help make it "worth the visit."

	FOOD	DECOR	SERVICE	COST

Cafe Medina 🅼 *Eclectic* | 24 | 24 | 21 | $28 |

Downtown | 556 Beatty St. (Dunsmuir St.) | 604-879-3114 |
www.medinacafe.com

Downtowners meet "rainy days" (and sunny ones) head-on with "addictive Belgian waffles", "divine toppings" and other "Eclectic dishes" at this "unique", all-day breakfast specialist (and "little brother to Chambar" next door) that also offers "delicious lunches" at "affordable prices"; cognoscenti "come early to beat the line-up" at the brick-lined room that closes at 4 PM.

🆕 Campagnolo *Italian* | – | – | – | M |

East Side | 1020 Main St. (bet. Millross & National Aves.) | 604-484-6018 |
www.campagnolorestaurant.ca

The focused style at this polished, vibrant salute to rustic Northern Italian cuisine from sommelier Tom Doughty and chef Robert Belcham has drawn crowds since day one to a rapidly revitalised, if still slightly gritty corner of the East Side; beyond the earth tones and exposed beams, diners find an affordable menu that includes open-face porchetta sandwiches, flank steaks with salsa verde and housemade meats from The Cure Salumi, located upstairs, matched with wines from a regional list stocked in a cosy rear bar.

Cannery, The *Seafood* | 23 | 22 | 23 | $58 |

East Side | 2205 Commissioner St. (Mcgill St.) | 604-254-9606 |
www.canneryseafood.com

"Come for the view, stay for the seafood" "presented with flair" and served by an "attentive", "friendly" staff say fans of this "iconic waterfront" East Sider and "longtime favourite" in a "nautical-industrial" setting; forget the "inconvenience of Port Security" and stop by before it enjoys its last "spectacular sunset" and closes forever in March 2010, after the Winter Olympics.

Cardero's Restaurant & Marine Pub *Pub Food* | 18 | 22 | 20 | $47 |

West End | 1583 Coal Harbour Quay (bet. Cardero & Nicola Sts.) |
604-669-7666

Situated "right on the waterfront" with an "awesome patio" and a "fantastic view of the mountains", this "casual" midpriced "West End hangout" is "more upscale pub than fine-dining venue"; regulars "have the wok squid" and advise "tourists" to "try the planked salmon", though some suggest just "belly up to the bar" and "skip the food."

Cassis Bistro ●◗⑤Ⓜ *French* | 20 | 19 | 19 | $36 |

Downtown | 420 W. Pender St. (bet. Homer & Richards Sts.) | 604-605-0420 | www.cassisvancouver.com

Bistrophiles seeking "authentic French" "comfort food" in "casual" digs head for this "charming", "funky" "heritage" room with "the smallest kitchen" in a "gastronomically bereft part" of Downtown; even if there's "not a lot of choice", partisans praise the attempt to use "all-organic" ingredients and the "high quality-to-price" ratio, plus a garden patio that's an "urban oasis"; N.B. a recent renovation is not reflected in the Decor score.

Century *Nuevo Latino* | ▽ 19 | 20 | 19 | $42 |

Downtown | 432 Richards St. (bet. Hastings & Pender Sts.) | 604-633-2700 | www.centuryhouse.ca

Hipsters head Downtown to this "dramatically" "beautiful" room in a "converted bank", with distressed walls, barrel-vaulted ceilings and marble floors, that offers "delicious" Nuevo Latino plates on its "something-for-everyone menu"; "friendly" service and prices that aren't too steep help keep things "comfortable."

Chambar Belgian Restaurant *Belgian* +5 | 26 | 24 | 24 | $53 |

Downtown | 562 Beatty St. (bet. Dunsmuir & Pender Sts.) | 604-879-7119 | www.chambar.com

"If you can't be in Brussels", this "cool" Downtown Belgian "does a good take" with "top-drawer moules frites", "inventive cocktails" and an "incredible selection" of ales; "even if it's a bit loud", there's "everything to like" about this "not too pricey" pre-theatre and "party scene", from the industrial decor featuring the works of local artists to an improved Service score for a "fantastic" staff that "treats you like family."

NEW Cibo Trattoria ⑤ *Italian* | 24 | 22 | 23 | $55 |

Downtown | Moda Hotel | 900 Seymour St. (Nelson St.) | 604-602-9570 | www.cibotrattoria.com

Chef Neil Taylor turns out "Italian like it was meant to be" at this Downtown trattoria adjoining the Moda Hotel, where his "sophisticated" dishes capture the "honest flavours" of "fresh" ingredients and the prix fixes "rock"; additional draws include "pro" sommelier-manager Sebastien Le Goff and an "unpretentious" vibe courtesy of "wonderful" "servers in jeans" and a rustic yet "stylish" setting featuring exposed timber and the original 1908 terra-cotta floor.

CinCin *Italian*

| 24 | 22 | 22 | $59 |

Downtown | 1154 Robson St. (bet. Bute & Thurlow Sts.) | 604-688-7338 | www.cincin.net

"Follow your nose" upstairs to the "wood-burning oven" of this "upscale" Downtown "Italian sensation" perched above "busy Robson Street", a "place to be seen" that "always delivers the goods" with "satisfying" fare, "helpful" service and a "warm, welcoming" room; even if it's "a bit pricey", most agree "you get what you pay for", especially when dining on the "hideaway patio"; N.B. a new chef arrived post-Survey.

Z Cioppino's Mediterranean Grill Z *Mediterranean*

| 28 | 23 | 25 | $74 |

Yaletown | 1133 Hamilton St. (bet. Davie & Helmcken Sts.) | 604-688-7466 | www.cioppinosyaletown.com

Pino Posteraro is a "true celebrity chef" assure fans who promise a "profound" "culinary adventure" at this Yaletown Mediterranean where "amazing" "modern and traditional fare" is delivered with "extraordinary service" from a "beautiful open kitchen" in the "elegant", earth-hued space; though the "price tag matches his lofty talent" and you might "bring an extra credit card" for the "extensive wine list", it's a "can't-miss dining experience"; N.B. the more rustic-looking Enoteca is next door.

NEW Circa Restaurant & Lounge ●M *Pacific NW*

| ∇ 18 | 20 | 21 | $46 |

Downtown | 1050 Granville St. (bet. Helmcken & Nelson Sts.) | 604-683-3311 | www.circarestolounge.com

Taking a decor cue from 18th-century Spain, this striking two-storey Downtown newcomer blends an elegant bar and comfy booths with its dining hall serving Pacific Northwest cuisine set below arches and soaring gold-leafed pillars; highlights range from wild salmon to crispy confit pork hock complemented by trendy cocktails and an all-British Columbia wine list.

	FOOD	DECOR	SERVICE	COST

Coast ● *Seafood* — 23 | 22 | 22 | $64

West End | 1054 Alberni St. (bet. Burrard & Thurlow Sts.) | 604-685-5010 | www.coastrestaurant.ca

"Bigger and more attractive" in its "fantastic new", "cool" Alberni Street location, this "lively" Downtown seafooder with a "hip" circular oyster and chowder bar "is a winner" for "focused, light" "fresh fish that never disappoints"; though nitpickers note it's "a bit overpriced" and "somewhat noisy", an "attentive, knowledgeable staff" plus the adjacent O Lounge add to the reasons most insist "it's worth it"; N.B. the Decor score might not reflect a mid-Survey move.

Cobre *Nuevo Latino* — 22 | 20 | 19 | $46

Gastown | 52 Powell St. (bet. Carrall & Columbia Sts.) | 604-669-2396 | www.cobrerestaurant.com

Nuevo Latino cuisine draws a "happening" crowd to this "friendly", "new-age tapas bar" decked out in brick-and-copper situated in "a Gastown that's starting to find its hipster vibe"; while amigos attest to the "reasonably" priced "innovative" fare, "big selection of tequilas" and "killer sangria" and adversaries find the portions "even smaller" than expected, all agree there's "not much else like it in the city."

Crave *American* — 21 | 17 | 19 | $37

East Side | 3941 Main St. (bet. 23rd & 24th Aves.) | 604-872-3663 | www.craveonmain.ca

Regulars "get in line" for New American "comfort food" "with an upscale twist" at this "unassuming", "deservedly popular" East Side "neighbourhood bistro"; even if it's "cramped when busy", advocates agree it's "always innovative" and "you get what you pay for" here, so "it's worth the wait", especially for the "patio garden out back in summer."

NEW Crave Beachside *Pacific NW* — 22 | 23 | 22 | $38

West Vancouver | 1362 Marine Dr. (bet. 13th St. & 14th Ave.) | 604-926-3332 | www.craveonmain.ca

"When the weather is right", surveyors "get a table on the patio" for an "amazing" "view of Ambleside Beach across to Stanley Park" at this Pacific Northwest bistro newcomer in West Vancouver; it's "larger than its Main Street sibling", and fans say the "well-done comfort food" has service to match, for a "delightful" experience that "doesn't break the bank."

	FOOD	DECOR	SERVICE	COST

C Restaurant *Seafood* — 25 | 24 | 24 | $81

Downtown | 2-1600 Howe St. (Beach Ave.) | 604-681-1164 |
www.crestaurant.com

"It's an A for C" cheer champions of chef Robert Clark's "impeccable",
"guilt-free", "sustainably sourced" seafood at this "premium"
Downtown shoreside room with vaulted ceilings and a wall of
windows; even if a few fret that it's "too expensive" and "trendy", most
concur the "professional, congenial" service and "unique" flavours
including a tasting menu "where cuisine and culture meet" are
"worth saving for."

Cru *Pacific NW* — 25 | 20 | 24 | $57

West Side | 1459 W. Broadway (bet. Granville & Hemlock Sts.) |
604-677-4111 | www.cru.ca

Grape groupies find a "nice surprise" in the "focused" Pacific
Northwest small plates and "stellar" prix fixe "deals" at this "consistently excellent" "gem" of a West Sider run by Mark Taylor, the
"charming" owner-sommelier who "gets it on all levels", starting with
a "thoughtful wine list"; even if it's "a bit cramped", the "attentive",
"helpful" staff assures an experience that's "not fussy", also making it
"perfect for a date."

NEW db Bistro Moderne *French* — 23 | 22 | 22 | $61

West Side | 2551 W. Broadway (bet. Larch & Trafalgar Sts.) | 604-739-7115 |
www.dbbistro.ca

Owner "Daniel Boulud knows" his stuff say fans, calling the
vaunted db Burger a "must-try" at this "glamorous", "well-cloned"
outpost of the Manhattan original that brings a "definite New York
vibe" to the West Side with its bistro "twists on French classics";
though a few find the "sleek decor" and prices a bit "too fancy",
"amazing" "local flavours" and generally "spot-on" service leave
most nodding "ain't cultural imperialism grand."

Delilah's Ⓜ *Pacific NW* — 20 | 21 | 22 | $49

West End | 1789 Comox St. (Denman St.) | 604-687-3424 | www.delilahs.ca

Seekers of "euthanasia via martini" still pack into the velvet banquettes
at this "energetic" West End "neighbourhood spot", which is especially popular "for a girls' night out"; if trend-watchers suggest the
otherwise "awesome" drinks list "needs updating", both the service

and the Pacific Northwest "prix fixe with choices" make for an "enjoyable" time, plus the "private booths" facilitate a "romantic dinner."

Diva at the Met *Pacific NW* | 26 | 23 | 25 | $72 |

Downtown | Metropolitan Hotel | 645 Howe St. (bet. Dunsmuir & W. Georgia Sts.) | 604-602-7788 | www.metropolitan.com

From "exquisitely prepared, beautifully plated" contemporary Pacific Northwest apps and entrees to "desserts to die for" to an "impeccable" staff that's "just friendly enough", this Downtown "dream" in the Metropolitan Hotel "has it all"; the contemporary setting of warm woods and marble is "elegant and comfortable", and cognoscenti conclude that yes, it's "expensive, but worth every penny."

Don Francesco Ristorante *Italian* | 24 | 20 | 23 | $58 |

Downtown | 860 Burrard St. (bet. Robson & Smithe Sts.) | 604-685-7770 | www.donfrancesco.ca

For "old-school Italian" "with a little opera thrown in", this classic Downtowner "is it", complete with "charming" servers who are "pros" and an "owner who often serenades"; the "well-appointed" Tuscan-inspired setting adds to the "lively" atmosphere, and regulars also go "especially for the game selections" and the "extensive" wine list.

🆕 Edge Social Grille, The ☻ *Eclectic* | – | – | – | M |
(aka The Edge)

Downtown | Best Western | 1100 Granville St. (Helmcken St.) | 604-681-3343 | www.theedgeongranville.com

Suits by day and locals at night pack into this smart Downtown Eclectic arrival in the Best Western, on the 'edge' of the Granville Street entertainment district; casual, affordable regional fare, well-chosen wines by the glass, snappy cocktails, late-night eats and a long bar with buzz add to the all-hours appeal.

Elixir Bistro *French* | 23 | 22 | 22 | $56 |

Yaletown | Opus Hotel | 350 Davie St. (Hamilton St.) | 604-642-0557 | www.elixirvancouver.ca

Chef Don Letendre blends "trendy nightspot with fine" French classics featuring "consistently current and local" ingredients at this "chic" Yaletown bistro "scene" in the "hip" Opus Hotel; though service can be "a tad slow", fans note that the "wine list is improving" and the "varied" moderately expensive menu "only gets better."

EN Japanese Restaurant Ⓜ *Japanese* | 24 | 20 | 21 | $42 |

West Side | 4422 W. 10th Ave. (bet. Sasamat & Trimble Sts.) | 604-730-0330 | www.encuisine.ca

Sushi-philes seek out this "quietly formal", "modern" West Side "neighbourhood gem" for its "expertly created and presented", "innovative" Japanese cuisine; devotees hail plates that are "works of art" at "good value" and applaud the "gracious" staff.

FigMint Restaurant & Lounge *European* | 19 | 21 | 18 | $53 |

West Side | Plaza 500 Hotel | 500 W. 12th Ave. (Cambie St.) | 604-875-3312 | www.figmintrestaurant.com

Now that the Canada Line has pulled in down the street, there's renewed interest in this "ambitious", "trendy", "modern yet comfortable" room in the West Side Plaza 500 Hotel where the chef Dennis Peckham has recently arrived to oversee a "pricey" Modern European menu featuring local ingredients; differing opinions on service indicate that "something's missing", but the "challenging space" is once again a "contender."

Fish House in Stanley Park *Seafood* | 22 | 22 | 22 | $50 |

West End | 8901 Stanley Park Dr. (Lagoon Dr.) | 604-681-7275 | www.fishhousestanleypark.com

"Those who love fish" "ask for a window seat" at this "family-friendly" Cape Cod–style "converted heritage house" in the heart of Stanley Park, where chef Karen Barnaby "excels" with her "healthy options" and other "impeccably fresh" seafood; even if it's "a bit tourist-y", most enjoy the "bucolic" setting and "non-rushed service" – especially for "Sunday brunch with mom", "wonderful afternoon tea" or to "view a Vancouver sunset."

Ⓩ Five Sails *French/Pacific NW* | 24 | 26 | 24 | $75 |

Downtown | Pan Pacific Hotel | 410-999 Canada Pl. (Howe St.) | 604-844-2855 | www.fivesails.ca

"Gorgeous" "views of the harbour and the lights of North Vancouver" coupled with chef-owner Ernst Dorfler's "sophisticated" Pacific NW-French fare makes for a "nearly magical evening" at this Downtown "hidden secret" located at (but owned separately from) the Pan Pacific Hotel; even if it's "on the pricey side", "outstanding service" and "beautiful presentation" help make it "worth the price of admission."

	FOOD	DECOR	SERVICE	COST

Fleuri French *dessert only*

| | 23 | 21 | 26 | $66 |

Downtown | Sutton Place Hotel | 845 Burrard St. (bet. Robson & Smithe Sts.) | 604-642-2900 | www.suttonplace.com

"It's better only in Paris" proclaim patrons of this *très* "comfortable", pricey French Downtown in the Sutton Place Hotel that offers "classic" fare and "stellar service" in an "old world-style" setting "with customers to match"; Thursday–Saturday nights, dessert devotees "move right to the chocolate buffet" that's "worth a trip on its own", and there's also the "occasional star sighting."

Flying Tiger, The *Asian*

| | 24 | 20 | 22 | $39 |

West Side | 2958 W. Fourth Ave. (Bayswater St.) | 604-737-7529 | www.theflyingtiger.ca

"Unique, delicious" fusion bites of "just-the-right-sized" tapas – including "highly recommended duck confit crêpes" – lure a legion to this "hidden West Side gem" serving "chef Tina Fineza's take on Asian street food"; "who cares about" the black-and-gold decor, with "quality" service, "reasonable prices" and "well-paired wines" in the equation, diners are "happy campers."

Fraîche Ⓜ *Pacific NW*

| | 24 | 26 | 25 | $62 |

West Vancouver | 2240 Chippendale Rd. (Boulder Ct.) | 604-925-7595 | www.fraicherestaurant.ca

"Stunning views" of the city skyline and the ocean are even "more spectacular than" chef Wayne Martin's "expertly prepared", "classic" Pacific Northwest plates at this "ultimate date" getaway located "high in the hills of West Vancouver (with a bill to match)"; "excellent" service in a "contemporary" white-tablecloth setting adds to an "exceptional experience" that the initiated insist is "worth the effort" "to cross the bridge."

Fuel Restaurant *Pacific NW*

| | 26 | 20 | 24 | $65 |

West Side | 1944 W. Fourth Ave. (bet. Cypress & Maple Sts.) | 604-288-7905 | www.fuelrestaurant.ca

"Fast for a few days" before dining at this West Side "mainstay locavore" suggest the "dazzled" denizens who vie for the "most coveted seats" across from chef Robert Belcham's "open kitchen" to watch the "obsessively sourced" Pacific Nortwest à la carte and tasting menus take shape; sommelier Tom Doughty oversees an "impressive cellar",

	FOOD	DECOR	SERVICE	COST

and the "service can be amazing" in the "chic" but "understated" room, so naturally, "it's expensive."

Globe @ YVR *Pacific NW*

| 22 | 20 | 22 | $60 |

Richmond | Fairmont Vancouver Airport Hotel | 3111 North Service Rd. (off Grant McConachie Way) | 604-207-5200 | www.fairmonthotels.com

"Watch the planes land" through the floor-to-ceiling windows at this "gorgeous" Pacific Northwester in the Fairmont Hotel at Richmond's Vancouver International; passengers "kill time tastefully between flights" at the "glistening bar" and say the "dependable" fare goes "well beyond the usual airport" grub and "never disappoints."

glowbal grill & satay bar ● *Eclectic*

| 21 | 20 | 20 | $46 |

Yaletown | 1079 Mainland St. (bet. Helmcken & Nelson Sts.) | 604-602-0835 | www.glowbalgrill.com

"Hipsters crane their necks to see" and "be seen" at this Yaletown "paparazzi favourite" with a 40-ft. bar that's known as much for its "trendy cocktail scene" as its "reliable" Eclectic fare; if detractors warn to "have your attitude on", others praise "brunch on the patio", the "quickly served", "good-value" lunch and "late-night apps"; N.B. AFTERglow, a 50-seat lounge, is in back.

Go Fish! Ⓜ *Seafood*

| 25 | 14 | 15 | $19 |

West Side | 1505 W. First Ave. (Fisherman's Wharf) | 604-730-5040

"Beware of hungry seagulls" at this West Side "open-air fish shack" where "in decent weather there's always a line" of "fellow seafood lovers" enduring "sassy" service for the "freshest" fin fare from "right off the dock"; even those lamenting "no indoor seating" admit "there's no better decor than the ocean" against which to enjoy the "signature tacos" and other plates for "cheap"; N.B. closes at 6:30 PM.

Goldfish Pacific Kitchen *Pacific NW*

| 20 | 22 | 21 | $55 |

Yaletown | 1118 Mainland St. (bet. Davie & Helmcken Sts.) | 604-689-8318 | www.goldfishkitchen.com

Whether surveyors are "dressed to the nines for a girls' night out" or hanging with the "hip crowd" for "after-work cocktails", this "gorgeous", "spacious" contemporary Yaletowner with "solid" Pacific Northwest fare is a "high-octane" ticket; though detractors detect "wannabe playas" and call it "a little expensive", "personable service" eases the negatives; N.B. a DJ spins Thursday–Saturday nights.

	FOOD	DECOR	SERVICE	COST

Gotham Steakhouse *Steak*

| | 24 | 23 | 24 | $74 |

Downtown | 615 Seymour St. (bet. Dunsmuir & W. Georgia Sts.) | 604-605-8282 | www.gothamsteakhouse.com

"Watch power brokers at work" at this "classic steakhouse" Downtown where "mega meat" "done to perfection" is delivered with "spot-on service" in a "larger-than-life" high-ceilinged setting filled with velvet and leather banquettes; just "pack a big wallet" for this "experience."

Griffins Restaurant *Pacific NW*

| | 22 | 19 | 22 | $47 |

Downtown | Fairmont Hotel Vancouver | 900 W. Georgia St. (Burrard St.) | 604-662-1900 | www.fairmonthotel.com

Downtown shoppers refuel at the "top-value" "all-you-can-eat buffets" ("desserts are worth it alone") at this Pacific Northwester also offering a regular menu amid "throwback" "decor matching the heritage building" of the Fairmont Hotel Vancouver; service is "all business", and while some call for "a makeover", others dub it the "prettiest room for a rainy afternoon."

Gyoza King ❶ *Japanese*

| | 24 | 14 | 16 | $25 |

West End | 1508 Robson St. (Nicola St.) | 604-669-8278

"You can't go wrong" at this "intimate little dumpling house" for "home-style Japanese" in the West End where even "chefs come to eat after work"; though "service and decor are no-frills", it's "affordable", plus devotees declare it's "worth every second of waiting for a spot."

Habit Lounge ❶ *Eclectic*

| | - | - | - | M |

East Side | 2610 Main St. (bet. E. 10th & 11th Aves.) | 604-877-8582 | www.habitlounge.ca

Those seeking Eclectic "comfort food with style" meet "friends" at this "hip", "funky" East Sider with "consistent" modern Canadian fare and "owners who treat you like family"; recently redecorated following a fire, it's destined to resume its place as a "favourite casual" "neighbourhood hangout"; sibling the Cascade Room is next door.

Hapa Izakaya ❶ *Japanese*

| | 22 | 20 | 20 | $39 |

West End | 1479 Robson St. (bet. Broughton & Nicola Sts.) | 604-689-4272
West Side | 1516 Yew St. (Cornwall Ave.) | 604-738-4272
www.hapaizakaya.com

"Adventurous" types "crowd" this "energetic" West Ender with a West Side sib that "brought izakaya to Vancouver" and where diners "mix and match" dishes "without paying an arm and a leg"; despite modern "decor that looks a little tired" to some, most "love the ambience", "friendly, sincere service" and "wonderful selection" of "tapas, often with a fusion spin."

Hart House, The ☒ Pacific NW

21 | 23 | 23 | $57

Burnaby | 6664 Deer Lake Ave. (bet. Deer Lake Pkwy. & Sperling Ave.) | 604-298-4278 | www.harthouserestaurant.com

"Old-fashioned" "charm" prevails at this "wonderful" Tudor-style heritage house in a "lakeside" Burnaby park setting where Pacific Northwest fare and "professional" service add up to a "classic dining" experience; though it's "a bit expensive", it's "worth it", "especially for Sunday brunch" or "special occasions" like the "parents' anniversary."

Hermitage, The French

25 | 22 | 24 | $60

Downtown | 115-1025 Robson St. (bet. Burrard & Thurlow Sts.) | 604-689-3237 | www.thehermitagevancouver.com

Francophiles seek out Hervé Martin's "cosy", "very European" "hidden treasure tucked away" Downtown in a Robson Street courtyard for its "unpretentious", "well-prepared" pricey French fare and service by "personable" "waiters who've been there forever"; regulars revel in the antique decorations and "old-world charm" with "no surprises", finding it all "lovely and romantic."

Herons Pacific NW

23 | 23 | 24 | $59

Downtown | Fairmont Waterfront Hotel | 900 Canada Place Way (bet. Burrard & Howe Sts.) | 604-691-1818 | www.fairmont.com

"Go early to get a window seat" at this "thoroughly delightful" Pacific Northwester in a contemporary room with floor-to-ceiling windows in the Fairmont Waterfront Hotel Downtown, where a "welcoming staff" provides "amazing service"; although some attribute the "high prices" to being "so close to the convention centre", regulars still get revved over the "delicious array" of brunch options.

Horizons on Burnaby Mountain Pacific NW

20 | 21 | 21 | $50

Burnaby | 100 Centennial Way (Burnaby Mountain Pkwy.) | 604-299-1155 | www.horizonsrestaurant.com

Surveyors "get away from the city" on Burnaby Mountain where the "beauty of the location" seduces at this Pacific Northwester with "lovely gardens" and "breathtaking", "faraway views of the harbour and Downtown"; if some "wish the fare could keep up" with the vistas, "service is friendly", and advocates attest it's "worth the trip to the top" – "especially at sunset."

Hy's Encore *Steak*

| 24 | 19 | 24 | $62 |

Downtown | 637 Hornby St. (bet. Dunsmuir & W. Georgia Sts.) | 604-683-7671 | www.hyssteakhouse.com

"Forget fancy" meateries, carnivores claim this Downtown "staple" remains the "quintessential" "men's-clubby", "old-style steakhouse" complete with "tableside Caesars", "melt-in-your-mouth" Canadian prime and "impeccable" service; true, the "Rat Pack decor" could "use a makeover", but fans "love the nostalgia" as much as the "cheese bread that should be on your bucket list."

Il Giardino di Umberto ⍗ *Italian*

| 26 | 25 | 25 | $67 |

Downtown | 1382 Hornby St. (Pacific St.) | 604-669-2422 | www.umberto.com

"Legendary" Umberto "never ceases to amaze" *amici* of this Downtown "old-school Italian" "culinary anchor" where the "sumptuous" fare, "impressive, professional service" and "romantic setting" transport patrons to a "Tuscan villa"; sure, it's a wallet-lightener, but between the "movers and shakers" and "movie stars", there's "always a scene", especially on the "pretty patio" populated with even "prettier people."

Imperial Chinese Seafood *Chinese*

| 23 | 20 | 21 | $42 |

Downtown | Marine Bldg. | 355 Burrard St. (W. Hastings St.) | 604-688-8191 | www.imperialrest.com

"Authentic Cantonese" with "taste and style" draws connoisseurs to this "elegant" Downtowner in the "gorgeous art deco" Marine Building where "Peking duck comes in many forms" and the "well-prepared" Chinese seafood is "right out of the tank"; service is "gracious" and "families, large groups" and others "go early" for "excellent dim sum" that some find "better than most in Hong Kong."

Irish Heather, The *Irish*

| 18 | 18 | 19 | $32 |

Gastown | 212 Carrall St. (bet. Cordova & Water Sts.) | 604-688-9779 | www.irishheather.com

"Guinness poured correctly" pleases pint purists at Gastown's "warm, welcoming" "modern take on an Irish bar", where the midpriced "fresh" "gastropub grub" (the "pot pie is a must") adds to the "convivial atmosphere"; nostalgists who lament that "it's not what it was" since its recent move are outnumbered by backers barking it's a "million times better"; N.B. "Shebeen whisky lounge out back" stocks 120 single malts.

Italian Kitchen ● *Italian*   20 | 20 | 19 | $52

Downtown | 1037 Alberni St. (bet. Burrard & Thurlow Sts.) | 604-687-2858 | www.theitaliankitchen.ca

"Sit at the bar" (it's 60 feet of marble) and "watch the action" at this "incredibly stylish" two-level Downtown Italian, where "trendy eye candy" decorates the "bustling" scene and no one "goes away hungry" after ordering the "amazing meatballs" and "pasta like grandma made"; detractors call it "overhyped" with uneven service, but most deem prices "fair", and even groups who have a "blast" suggest "bring earplugs."

Joe Fortes *Seafood/Steak* #10   22 | 21 | 22 | $55

Downtown | 777 Thurlow St. (bet. Alberni & Robson Sts.) | 604-669-1940 | www.joefortes.ca

Seafood aficionados tout the "wonderful oyster bar" while carnivores carve into "fabulous, huge steaks", all served by a "cheerful staff" at this Downtown American-style "classic" surf 'n' turfer named after the first local lifeguard; it's "always popular after work", and its rooftop patio offers a "view", a green "living wall" and a fireplace, but be warned – "you can easily spend all day there"; N.B. there's a pianist nightly.

Jules Bistro ⊠Ⓜ *French*   21 | 21 | 19 | $44

Gastown | 216 Abbott St. (bet. Cordova & Water Sts.) | 604-669-0033 | www.julesbistro.ca

Situated "in the heart of" "historic Gastown", this "very Parisian bistro" boasts "classic decor with black-and-white tiles and small tabletops" as a backdrop for "simple French country cooking"; though service is "spotty", the antique piano and bar and "live music Saturday nights" lend a "cosy, romantic" feel, plus it's "a lot cheaper" than "a trip to France."

Kalamata Greek Taverna Ⓜ *Greek*   21 | 16 | 20 | $32

West Side | 388 W. Broadway (Yukon St.) | 604-872-7050

"No one goes away hungry" from this long-standing West Side taverna where "roast lamb and other Greek specialties" "like grandma used to make" pair up with "attentive service" in a rustic setting with white stucco and wood floors; adding to the appeal are moderate prices, and usually a "doggy bag to enjoy a second delicious meal at home."

☒ Keg Steakhouse & Bar *Steak*

| 20 | 17 | 19 | $47 |

Burnaby | 4510 Stillcreek Ave. (Willingdon Ave.) | 604-294-4626 ◐
Downtown | 595 Hornby St. (Dunsmuir St.) | 604-687-4044
Downtown | 742 Thurlow St. (bet. Alberni & Robson Sts.) | 604-685-4388
Granville Island | 1499 Anderson St. (bet. Duranleau & Johnston Sts.) | 604-685-4735 ◐
New Westminster | 800 Columbia St. (8th St.) | 604-524-1381
Richmond | 11151 No. 5 Rd. (bet. Horseshoe Way & Steveston Hwy.) | 604-272-1399
Surrey | 15146 100th Ave. (152nd St.) | 604-583-6700 ◐
Surrey | 7948 120th St. (76th Ave.) | 604-591-6161
West Vancouver | Park Royal South Mall | 800 Marine Dr. (Taylor Way) | 604-925-9126 ◐
NEW **Yaletown** | 1011 Mainland St. (Nelson St.) | 604-633-2534
www.kegsteakhouse.com

Meat mavens "craving" a "standard steak" maintain this "Canadian success story" chophouse chain "never gets it wrong" with its "*Flintstones*-size servings" at "reasonable prices"; fans praise the "consistent quality" of the fare and while "atmosphere and crowds vary widely by location" (Yaletown is a "new hot spot"), most still return for "friendly service" and "good value."

Kingyo ◐ *Japanese*

| 26 | 23 | 24 | $39 |

West End | 871 Denman St. (bet. Barclay & Haro Sts.) | 604-608-1677 | www.kingyo-izakaya.com

"Inventive", "eclectic" plates of "hip, well-prepared Japanese tapas" lure partyers to this "highly entertaining" (like to be shouted at?) mid-priced izakaya "tucked away in" the West End; "exotic drinks" from a bar resembling a temple are served by a "perky", "sweet" staff that "explains every dish in detail" while "having a blast", all contributing to the "upbeat" "Tokyo vibe."

Kirin Mandarin *Chinese*

| 25 | 19 | 20 | $41 |

Downtown | 1166 Alberni St. (bet. Bute & Thurlow Sts.) | 604-682-8833 | www.kirinrestaurant.com

"For Peking duck" and dim sum of "exceptional quality and variety", regulars recommend this Downtown stalwart as the "place to go" for "savoury, fresh", "authentic" Chinese fare; though the "setting is uneventful", it "hums" with "lively atmosphere", and the "friendly, helpful staff" and "decent prices" help make it "consistently one of the best."

Kirin Seafood *Chinese*   24 | 18 | 20 | $41

Coquitlam | Henderson Pl. | 1163 Pinetree Way (bet. Glen Dr. & Lincoln Ave.) | 604-944-8833
New Westminster | Starlight Casino | 350 Gifford St. (Boyd St.) | 604-528-8833
Richmond | Three West Ctr. | 7900 Westminster Hwy., 2nd fl. (bet. Minoru Blvd. & No. 3 Rd.) | 604-303-8833
West Side | City Sq. | 555 W. 12th Ave., 2nd fl. (Cambie St.) | 604-879-8038
www.kirinrestaurant.com

"The freshest, tastiest seafood", "divine dim sum" and "refined takes on classics" lure Sinophiles to this Chinese quartet where "weekly chef creations ensure something new every time"; service is "attentive", and the "huge", "always packed" rooms will "make you swear you're in Hong Kong."

Kitanoya Guu ◗ *Japanese*   26 | 17 | 20 | $33

Downtown | 105-375 Water St. (W. Cordova St.) | 604-685-8682
Downtown | 1698 Robson St. (Bidwell St.) | 604-685-8678
Downtown | 838 Thurlow St. (bet. Robson & Smithe Sts.) | 604-685-8817
www.guu-izakaya.com

"More adventurous eaters" revel in the "innovative" small-plates "Japanese pub fare" at this trio of "rowdy izakayas" where the "delectable bites" and "whimsical, cheap cocktails" are presented by a "staff that hollers out greetings and orders" while seeming "genuinely happy to serve you"; despite having "to wait for a seat" and decor that's "not pretty", the experience "never disappoints."

Kobe *Japanese/Steak*   22 | 19 | 21 | $65

Downtown | 1042 Alberni St. (bet. Burrard & Thurlow Sts.) | 604-684-2451 | www.koberestaurant.com

"Tender" Alberta beef and seafood is "cooked right in front of you" teppanyaki-style by "chefs with acrobatic knives" at this Downtown "classic" Japanese steakhouse that fans find "entertaining time after time"; detractors suggest "portions could be more generous for the prices", though all agree that the country-inn setting and "animated staff" are "enjoyable."

	FOOD	DECOR	SERVICE	COST

Z La Belle Auberge 🆂🅼 *French* **28 | 23 | 26 | $68**

Ladner | 4856 48th Ave. (49th St.) | 604-946-7717 | www.labelleauberge.com

One of Vancouver's "best-kept secrets" and rated No. 1 for Food in this Survey, this "world-class" French from "legendary chef" Bruno Marti delivers "divine", "deep flavours" via "exquisite", "seasonal menus" served in a "beautiful", "romantic" 1905 Victorian heritage house tucked away in the Ladner "countryside"; "charming", "impeccable" service completes a "delightful" if pricey dining experience that leaves surveyors who "could rhapsodize endlessly" sighing "I only wish I lived in the neighbourhood."

NEW La Brasserie ● *French/German* *Key Newcomer* **23 | 20 | 22 | $45**

West End | 1091 Davie St. (Thurlow St.) | 604-568-6499 | www.labrasserievancouver.com

New to the West End's Davie Village, this "intimate", warm and woody spot serving French and German specialties has "fast" become a "busy" "local favourite" for its "awesome", "classic" brasserie fare, "wine selection", "impressive beer list" and "genuine", "welcoming staff"; reservations aren't taken, but it offers "good value" and it's "well worth the wait" to "sit at the bar" and channel "Montréal or Europe."

La Buca *Italian* **26 | 17 | 22 | $50**

West Side | 4025 Macdonald St. (bet. 24th & 25th Aves.) | 604-730-6988 | www.labuca.ca

"Go early and often" for chef Andrey Durbach's "muscular" Italian dishes "that aren't afraid to go bold" with "simple, elegant, amazing flavours" root regulars of this "shoebox-sized" trattoria "secreted away" on the West Side; a "most excellent wine list" and "gracious, attentive service" contribute to the "heartwarming" atmosphere and "value", but the "handful" of seats dictate "you must have a reservation."

NEW L'Altro Buca *Italian* **26 | 22 | 24 | $57**

West End | 1906 Haro St. (Gilford St.) | 604-683-6912 | www.altrobuca.ca

Located on an "unexpected corner of the West End", chef Andrey Durbach's recently redone second location of La Buca (fka Parkside) has quickly become a "neighbourhood hangout" considered a "value" for its "lively menu" of "delicious" Italian dishes and "wine choices" delivered by a "cheerful" staff; the "charming room" indoors is "perfect for a romantic interlude" while the "outside terrace" is made for "sipping prosecco on hot summer nights."

NEW La Quercia ☒ Italian

25 | 19 | 24 | $55

West Side | 3689 W. Fourth Ave. (Alma St.) | 604-676-1007 | www.laquercia.ca

Sandwiched "between a bank and a flower shop", this West Side "gem" of a "small room with a big heart" offers "deceptively simple yet simply delicious" Italian dishes from an "inspired", "hugely talented kitchen" that are delivered by a "knowledgeable, patient staff"; it may be "difficult to get in", but diners sitting "cheek-by-jowl" attest it "deserves the rave reviews."

La Régalade ☒☒ French

26 | 20 | 23 | $50

West Vancouver | 102-2232 Marine Dr. (bet. 22nd & 23rd Sts.) | 604-921-2228 | www.laregalade.com

"Wonderful, rustic" "traditional French favourites" of "top quality" reign at this "homey", "comforting" West Vancouver bistro where "meat dishes are king" and the "friendly, helpful staff" contributes to the "authentic" ambience; "portions are enormous" ("and you will try to finish every last bite"), still, those "not counting calories" advise "try to save room" for the "beautiful desserts."

La Terrazza Italian

25 | 25 | 26 | $68

Yaletown | 1088 Cambie St. (Pacific Blvd.) | 604-899-4449 | www.laterrazza.ca

"Long-established" as a "favourite with locals", this "stylish", "top-end" Yaletown Italian with improved scores in all areas offers "flawless service", "elegant cuisine" and a "serious wine list" say devotees declaring "every detail is looked after"; the "beautiful, spacious" quarters featuring 30-ft. ceilings and a seasonal patio breathe a "wonderful ambience" and befit "bringing your loved one."

NEW Latitude on Main Eclectic
(aka Latitude)

- | - | - | M

East Side | 3250 Main St. (bet. 16th & 17th Aves.) | 604-875-6246

At this new East Side Eclectic with a dash of Nuevo Latino on blossoming Main Street, hipsters hang at the gorgeous white Carrera marble bar while sipping BC and globe-trotting vintages or cocktails; the clean, minimalist design is a backdrop for carefully sourced local or-

FOOD | DECOR | SERVICE | COST

ganic and sustainable ingredients on a menu that yields plenty of shared plates and well-priced mains.

Ƶ Le Crocodile Ƶ *French*　　　27 | 23 | 27 | $78

Downtown | 100-909 Burrard St. (Smithe St.) | 604-669-4298 | www.lecrocodilerestaurant.com

Everyone "wants to be a regular" at Michel Jacob's "refined" Downtown French where "phenomenal" "classic cuisine" "with flair" combines with "impeccable service" for an experience that's "pure class"; acolytes aver the "high-end", "extensive, alluring menu" and "excellent wine list" are "the utmost" and "draw you like a magnet" to the "warm", "upscale" bistro setting complete with banquettes and mirrors.

Le Gavroche *French*　　　22 | 20 | 23 | $65

West End | 1616 Alberni St. (bet. Bidwell & Cardero Sts.) | 604-685-3924 | www.legavroche.ca

"Beautiful French atmosphere", "elegant", "traditional" cuisine in "portions large enough to please" and "wonderful", "attentive service" draw Francophiles to this "romantic", "cosy" spot in a "quiet" "old Victorian West End house"; with an "astonishing list of Bordeaux and California cult" labels including "tons of hidden gems", oenophiles opine "if the wine makes your meal, this is your place" – leaving some sighing, if only they could "afford it more often."

NEW Les Faux *Key Newcomer*　　　23 | 22 | 22 | $41
Bourgeois Bistro ● Ⓜ *French*

East Side | 663 E. 15th Ave. (Fraser St.) | 604-873-9733 | www.lesfauxbourgeois.com

Voyageurs to this "popular" "little" "gem of a French bistro" on the East Side discover "unpretentious fare" at "affordable prices"; though some find the "friendly" service "inconsistent", everyone at the "hopping bar" – from the "younger crowd" to "hipsters" to locals of this "untrendy neighbourhood" – agrees it has "great energy."

Lift *Pacific NW*　　　18 | 25 | 18 | $56

West End | 333 Menchions Mews (Bay Shore Dr.) | 604-689-5438 | www.liftbarandgrill.com

"Watch the seaplanes land" thanks to the "stellar views of Coal Harbour" at this "hip space" in the West End that's an otherwise "serviceable" Pacific Northwester; though the pricey fare "doesn't live up to the tony structure" and decor featuring a backlit onyx bar, the "people are cool" and the "deck is amazing."

Lolita's South of the Border Cantina ❶ *Mexican*

22 | 16 | 20 | $37

West End | 1326 Davie St. (bet. Broughton & Jervis Sts.) | 604-696-9996 | www.lolitasrestaurant.com

"Go early" or late "to avoid the wait" at this "tiny" but "trendy" mid-priced West Ender "in the heart of Davie Village" offering "cunning combinations of taste" that are "not your common take on Mexican" (some "question which border it's south of"); even if it's "cramped" with "not entirely authentic" tiki-style decor, for "fast service", "amazing margaritas" and "laughter", it's "fabulous."

Lombardo's Ristorante *Italian/Pizza*

20 | 13 | 18 | $30

East Side | Il Mercato | 120-1641 Commercial Dr. (E. 1st Ave.) | 604-251-2240 | www.lombardos.ca

Pie-sani in pursuit of "thin-crust", wood-oven pizza swear this East Side emporium "strangely located in a shopping mall" is the "place to go" for "traditional Italian home cooking"; even if the room looks "stuck in the '70s", "service is attentive and prices are reasonable"; N.B. the Downtown location at 970 Smithe Street has recently reopened as Pacifico Pizzeria and Ristorante.

Lumière Ⓜ *French*

26 | 23 | 25 | $108

West Side | 2551 W. Broadway (bet. Larch & Trafalgar Sts.) | 604-739-8185 | www.lumiere.ca

Those seeking a "sublime", "divinely decadent" experience make the pilgrimage to owner Daniel Boulud's "warm, inviting" modern West Side destination French, where the "epitome of Vancouver fine dining" is "exquisite, yet as understated as the name" and enhanced by "attentive", "not intrusive service"; while a nostalgic few pine "it's not the same without (Iron Chef) Rob" Feenie, most exult that the new team "meets expectations", even if it all comes at a "huge price."

NEW Maenam ❶ⓈⓂ *Thai* Key Newcomer

26 | 21 | 24 | $43

West Side | 1938 W. Fourth Ave. (bet. Cypress & Maple Sts.) | 604-730-5579 | www.maenam.ca

"Throw out your preconceptions and try this" "upmarket" new West Side Thai, a "bright spot" in Kitsilano offering "authentic, flavourful" plates "expertly executed" by chef-owner Angus An along with "elegant service" in a "modern", warm room with dark bamboo walls; even if some say "portions are small", most deem "prices reasonable" and find that the "flair" of the fare "complements a cool cocktail list."

Marcello *Italian/Pizza*
22 | **17** | **16** | **$32**

East Side | 1404 Commercial Dr. (Kitchener St.) | 604-215-7760

Patrons praise this "consistently solid", "classy but comfortable" mid-priced East Side Italian for its "homemade" pasta and "wood-oven pizzas" from a huge brick oven; portions are so generous "you'll probably have enough for lunch the next day", though service can be "so slow" some "wonder if" dinner is "arriving from Italy."

NEW Market by Jean-Georges ⑤ *French*
26 | **25** | **24** | **$67**

Downtown | Shangri-La Hotel | 1128 W. Georgia St. (bet. Bute & Thurlow Sts.) | 604-689-1120 | www.shangri-la.com

Jean-Georges Vongerichten's "hip and happening" new outpost for "modern French cuisine" in the Shangri-La Hotel has already become a "home-run" "hot spot Downtown", offering fare that "lives up to the hype" in "gorgeous surroundings" – including an "impressive dining room", cafe with fireplace and "wonderful outdoor patio"; disciples declare that "servers know their menu", and though it's generally "not inexpensive", the "lunchtime prix fixe is a bargain."

Maurya Indian Cuisine *Indian*
21 | **22** | **19** | **$39**

West Side | 1643 W. Broadway (bet. Fir & Pine Sts.) | 604-742-0622 | www.mauryaindiancuisine.com

When they "can't get into Vij's", surveyors head for this midpriced West Side "little-known gem" where "different styles of Indian cuisine" are presented amid "inviting decor" that combines classic and contemporary touches; regulars return for the "creative use of spices", "friendly (but not overly so) service" and the daily lunch buffet with "plenty of choices for both vegetarians and carnivores."

Me & Julio ❶ *Mexican*
17 | **18** | **18** | **$34**

East Side | 2095 Commercial Dr. (5th Ave.) | 604-696-9997 | www.meandjulio.ca

"Inventive but approachable", this modestly priced sibling to Lolita's is "worth a visit" say amigos of the "funky" East Side Mexican "neighbourhood spot on The Drive" with "something for everyone" on the menu from sarsaparilla-glazed ribs to tofu; even those feeling the fare "lacks punch" still "go with friends for drinks" and enjoy the "youthful", "lively atmosphere" with star-shaped lights overhead.

Memphis Blues Barbeque House *BBQ*

| 21 | 11 | 13 | $26 |

East Side | 1342 Commercial Dr. (bet. Charles & Kitchener Sts.) | 604-215-2599
Kelowna | 289 Bernard Ave. (Water St.) | 250-868-3699
North Vancouver | 1629 Lonsdale Ave. (16th St.) | 604-929-3699
NEW Surrey | Grandview Corners Mall | 2443-161A St. (24th Ave.) | 604-531-8005
West Side | 1465 W. Broadway (bet. Granville & Hemlock Sts.) | 604-738-6806
www.memphisbluesbbq.com

"Bring a big appetite" for "beef brisket you'd sell your mother for" at this multi-branch BBQ "carnivore heaven" where those of the protein persuasion forgive the "minimal decor and service" for "some of the best pulled pork this side of the border" and other "smoky" fare; but "you gotta love messy", so "don't bring a date unless you know you're sexy covered in sauce."

NEW Miku Restaurant *Japanese*

| - | - | - | E |

Downtown | 1055 W. Hastings St. (Burrard St.) | 604-568-3900 | www.mikurestaurant.com

Aficionados of *aburi* (flame-grilled sushi) reckon this "pricey" newly arrived Downtowner might be the "only place" in town offering the Japanese specialty, and it does so in a dramatic setting featuring a pebble floor, stainless-steel bar and soaring glass 'clouds'; early reports are mixed, but mention is made of "congenial service" and "artisan sake" (made on Granville Island), along with grilled salmon and beef from an extensive, seafood-centric menu.

Mistral Bistro ⊠ Ⓜ *French*

| 24 | 19 | 26 | $50 |

West Side | 2585 W. Broadway (bet. Larch & Trafalgar Sts.) | 604-733-0046 | www.mistralbistro.ca

"When the budget rules out a trip to the South of France" surveyors "take comfort" in this casual West Side "classic French bistro" with "wonderful Provençal fare" and "hospitable", "personal service"; patrons who choose it for "dining with friends" say it "delivers" "genuine" Gallic "feel" "without the hype", plus "excellent value", especially at the <u>lunch prix fixe.</u>

NEW Mis Trucos ● Ⓜ *Mediterranean*   - | - | - | E

West End | 1141 Davie St. (bet. Bute & Thurlow Sts.) | 604-566-3960 | www.mistrucos.ca

Tucked away up a flight of stairs in a lovingly restored old home in the heart of the West End's Davie Village, this casual small-plates specialist combines authentic, traditional Mediterranean tapas, such as white anchovy with hot peppers and olive, with Pacific Northwest influences; simplicity of style and attention to sound ingredients produce a plethora of flavours in dishes such as white truffle and lobster risotto, while the bar focuses on pouring classic cocktails and Spanish sips.

Montri's Thai Ⓜ *Thai*   23 | 17 | 22 | $36

West Side | 3629 W. Broadway (bet. Alma & Dunbar Sts.) | 604-738-9888 | www.montri-thai.com

"Fabulous", "fresh" Thai fare at "reasonable prices" is the draw at this "reliable" West Side "standby" with a "friendly, helpful staff"; though it "hasn't changed much", and the decor is basically "generic", devotees declare it has "maintained its outstanding quality."

Moustache Café ● Ⓜ *Mediterranean*   23 | 21 | 22 | $47

North Vancouver | 129 W. Second. St. (bet. Chesterfield & Lonsdale Aves.) | 604-987-8461 | www.moustachecafe.ca

"Sophisticated" "consistently excellent" Mediterranean fare in a "stylish setting" attracts surveyors to this "lovely little place" "hidden away among the residential towers of North Vancouver"; since its 2007 move, the new, contemporary setting is "fantastic", plus service is still "with a smile", making it "well worth the trip."

Nat's New York Pizzeria *Pizza*   22 | 10 | 15 | $15

West End | 1080 Denman St. (bet. Comox & Pendrell Sts.) | 604-642-0777
West Side | 2684 W. Broadway (bet. Stephens & Trafalgar Sts.) | 604-737-0707
www.natspizza.com

It's "the closest to a New York slice around" at this West Side and West End duo that's again the No. 1 Bang for the Buck in the Vancouver Survey for its "superb", "crisp", "thin-crust" pizza with "zesty sauce" and "lots of different toppings"; the digs aren't especially conducive to "lingering"

	FOOD	DECOR	SERVICE	COST

(some suggest "takeout") and "service? - let's just say it comes with some attitude"; still, pie-eyed patrons exit "doing the happy dance."

NEW Nook 🛇 *Italian* — | — | — | M

West End | 781 Denman St. (bet. Alberni & Robson Sts.) | 604-568-4554 | www.nookrestaurant.ca

Be prepared for a possible wait at this popular, casual West End newcomer that's already won a solid reputation for its rustic-but-subtle Italian cuisine based on authentic recipes and soundly sourced ingredients; patrons are packing the unpretentious room for the likes of prosciutto and arugula thin-crust pizza or fresh-daily handmade gnocchi, served with affordable wines from a gently adventurous regional list.

Nu ☮ *Eclectic* 21 | 21 | 19 | $53

Downtown | 1661 Granville St. (Pacific St.) | 604-646-4668 | www.whatisnu.com

Located "right on the water", it's "hard to beat the deck" at this "sleek", "chic" Downtown "hideaway" that offers "innovative", "sustainable, fresh" Eclectic fare against a "stunning view of False Creek"; though quibblers quip it's "pricey" and "not so 'nu' anymore", the majority says it's "like being on a cruise ship" and a "must for out-of-town guests", "to catch a sunset" or romantic "dining in a special setting."

NEW Nuba Restaurant *Lebanese* 24 | 24 | 21 | $28

Gastown | 207-B W. Hastings St. (Cambie St.) | 604-688-1655

Nuba Café *Lebanese*

Downtown | 1206 Seymour St. (Davie St.) | 778-371-3266 | www.nuba.ca

"Just a hint of glam" distinguishes this new Gastown Lebanese that offers "fairly priced", "wholesome", "organic fare" along with "knowledgeable" service; "film and fashion industry" types decorate the "cool", "laid-back setting" that channels "Beirut in the '40s" and is "more comfortable" than the "tiny" original Downtown cafe's "minimal" digs.

Ocean Club ▽ 22 | 24 | 20 | $47

Restaurant & Lounge ☮Ⓜ *Pacific NW*

West Vancouver | 105-100 Park Royal (Bridge St.) | 604-926-2326 | www.theoceanclub.ca

"Dark, loud and upbeat", this "modern" West Vancouver dining lounge offers Pacific Northwest fare amid white couches, slate pillars and exotic wood; the service can be "decidedly casual" for such an "upscale" setting, and with a Wednesday–Sunday DJ, some suggest it's more of a "local hangout" than a dinner destination worthy of "crossing the bridge."

O'Doul's Restaurant & Bar *Pacific NW*

22 | 20 | 22 | $44

Downtown | Listel Hotel | 1300 Robson St. (Jervis St.) | 604-661-1400 | www.odoulsrestaurant.com

"Jazz is the thing" at this "classy" but casual Pacific Northwester in the Listel Hotel that's a "lively", "long-standing favourite" "oasis" for West Enders; regulars who've been "going for years" return for "amazing live music" nightly with "better-than-expected" fare and service adding up to "good value."

Pajo's ⊄ *Seafood*

21 | 12 | 14 | $15

Port Moody | Rocky Point Park | 2800 Murray St. (Moody St.) | 604-469-2289

Steveston | The Wharf | 12351 Third Ave. (Bayview St.) | Richmond | 604-272-1588

Steveston | Garry Point Park (Chatham St.) | Richmond | 604-204-0767

www.pajos.com

"How much better can it get?" ask finny fans of these "funky little" cheap seafood "institutions" on the waterfront in Steveston and Port Moody where "people-watching seagulls" add "ambience" to a meal of some of the "best fish 'n' chips" "in the Lower Mainland"; devotees of "deep-fried goodness" keep the "casual outdoor seating" "always crowded in summer" (and call ahead in winter to assure it's open).

Pear Tree, The Ⓢ Ⓜ *Continental*

25 | 23 | 25 | $64

Burnaby | 4120 E. Hastings St. (bet. Carleton & Gilmore Aves.) | 604-299-2772 | www.peartreerestaurant.net

It may be "a bit off the beaten path", but this "small, inviting" "gem in the heart of North Burnaby" is a "must-visit" for its "fresh", "seasonal" Continental cuisine; "minimalist decor is inviting enough" say locavores hailing chef-owner Scott Jaeger as one who "never ceases to amaze" with "flawless execution", and praising a staff that delivers "rock-steady", "personal" service."

	FOOD	DECOR	SERVICE	COST

Pied-à-Terre *French* | 24 | 21 | 23 | $49 |

West Side | 3369 Cambie St. (bet. 17th & 18th Aves.) | 604-873-3131 |
www.pied-a-terre-bistro.ca

There's "no fusion, nothing weird" at this "awesome" West Side bistro (from the La Buca team) that's a "small room with big flavours" where surveyors who "order the prix fixe prepare to be stuffed" with "authentic French cuisine"; even if the "seating's a little tight" and it "fills up quickly", it's "like being in Paris", only with "amazing" service and "reasonable prices" – and it's even more "perfect with your honey."

NEW Ping's Cafe Ⓜ *Japanese* | 19 | 20 | 15 | $32 |

East Side | 2702 Main St. (11th Ave.) | 604-873-2702 |
www.pingscafe.ca

"Hipsters" seeking a "different take on Japanese" head to this "little gem" on the East Side for "down-home" dishes "with Canadian influence" plus "good value"; izakaya aficionados agree it "may not look like much on the outside", but inside the mismatched decor is "cool" enough for the "local art stars", so all in all, "how could you not like it?"

NEW Pourhouse ◑ *Eclectic* | ▽ 18 | 20 | 18 | $30 |

Gastown | 162 Water St. (bet. Abbott & Cambie Sts.) | 604-568-7022 |
www.pourhousevancouver.com

Not surprisingly, at this Gastown Eclectic newcomer from chef Chris Irving (ex West) and bartender-about-town Jay Jones (ex West and Voya) the focus is very much on the long bar in a historically sensitive and sensual setting; however, beyond Jones' hallmark Gold Fashioned made with bourbon, maple syrup and bitters, the kitchen delivers such affordable homespun treats as whole campfire trout and apple tatin with whisky caramel.

Provence Marinaside *French* | 23 | 22 | 22 | $52 |

Yaletown | 1177 Marinaside Cres. (Davie St.) | 604-681-4144 |
www.provencevancouver.com

"No need to travel to Nice" when you can "take a stroll on the boardwalk after dinner" at Yaletown's "fabulous waterfront" French, where "casual or dressy", "you can't go wrong" with a "lovely selection of antipasti" and "excellent" seafood; flaneurs fixate on the "deep wine list" and "professional service" and insist that with its "wonderful" "patio for people-watching", it's "definitely worth a visit."

	FOOD	DECOR	SERVICE	COST

Provence Mediterranean   25 | 19 | 22 | $49
Grill *French/Mediterranean*
West Side | 4473 W. 10th Ave. (bet. Sasamat & Trimble Sts.) | 604-222-1980 |
www.provencevancouver.com

"Local loyal" patrons profess the "heavenly" French-Mediterranean cuisine's "not trying to be nouveau" at this "trusty" "neighbourhood" West Sider with "serious talent" in the kitchen; service that's "quick, polite and attentive" in a "well-spaced room with comfortable seating" plus a patio that's a "delight on a sunny day" are additional draws.

Q4 *Italian*   25 | 21 | 23 | $58
(fka Quattro on Fourth)
West Side | 2611 W. Fourth Ave. (Trafalgar St.) | 604-734-4444 |
www.quattroonfourth.com

"First-class", "elegant homestyle" Italian fare has made this West Side "institution" a "perennial winner" with an "amazing menu" that's explained by the "unpretentious", "knowledgeable staff"; improved scores verify "guaranteed consistency and quality" that "never disappoints", so even if it's "a bit pricey", it's popular for "dining with friends."

Raincity Grill *Pacific NW*   24 | 20 | 23 | $58
West End | 1193 Denman St. (Morton Ave.) | 604-685-7337 |
www.raincitygrill.com

Locavores laud the "impeccable", "fresh" Pacific Northwest cuisine at this "venerable" West End "legend" where the "stylish, innovative" fare "showcases local ingredients" and "knowledgeable" "servers can chat about the dishes" and "perfect pairings" from the regional wine list; the "100-Mile Tasting Menu" underscores a "well-deserved reputation", and though decor is "rather minimalist", "incredible sunset views of English Bay" are "an added bonus."

NEW Refinery, The ◐ *Eclectic*   ▽ 20 | 23 | 17 | $41
Downtown | 1115 Granville St. (bet. Davis & Helmcken Sts.) | 604-687-7474 |
www.therefineryvancouver.com

Small tastes of all things local are meant for sharing at this upstairs Downtown Eclectic that takes its environmental responsibilities seriously both on and off the plate; the cosy decor of recycled materials plus local wines and creative cocktails add up to an unpretentious evening that won't break the bank; Sip Resto Lounge is downstairs.

	FOOD	DECOR	SERVICE	COST

NEW Revel Room, The ● M _Eclectic_
▽ 20 | 19 | 21 | $40

Gastown | 238 Abbott St. (bet. Corodova & Water Sts.) | 604-687-4088 |
www.revelroom.ca

"Don't take gramps" to this "funky, loud" Gastown "restaurant industry hangout", where the "after-work" crowd gathers for cocktails that "go down fast" plus "decent" Eclectic fare at a "decent price" from a kitchen that's "open late"; the split-level quarters and "hospitality" stoke a "lively atmosphere" that's "perfect for a night out" – complete with "eye candy"; P.S. there's "live jazz on Sundays" at brunch.

Rodney's Oyster House _Seafood_
24 | 17 | 21 | $54

Yaletown | 1228 Hamilton St. (bet. Davie & Drake Sts.) | 604-609-0080 |
www.rodneysoysterhouse.com

"Between the shucking, music and people-watching", there's ample "entertainment" at this "raucous" Yaletowner that bivalve fans dub "oyster heaven in a fish shack–style dump"; the "talented servers" might be "a little too casual", which "matches the decor, if not the prices", but the "seafood couldn't be fresher if you hauled it in yourself."

NEW r.tl ● _Eclectic_
▽ 25 | 20 | 21 | $52

Yaletown | 1130 Mainland St. (bet. Davie & Helmcken Sts.) | 604-638-1550 |
www.r.tl   _Key Newcomer_

"Menus that change – featuring three regional world cuisines at a time – result in "innovative" Eclectic "tapas-sized share plates" at this "trendy" Yaletown newcomer; diners who "figure out how to get in" the "sliding-glass door that's like something from _Star Trek_" are greeted with "snappy service" and 30 wine options from a "cutting-edge by-the-glass system" plus an "attention to detail", leaving surveyors "loving the concept."

Salade de Fruits Café ⓢ M ⮔ _French_
23 | 12 | 20 | $34

West Side | French Cultural Ctr. | 1551 W. Seventh Ave. (bet. Fir & Granville Sts.) | 604-714-5987 | www.saladedefruits.com

"Formidable moules frites" and other "classic bistro fare" lures Francophiles to this "cosy little" West Side "sweet spot" with "cheerful" service" "tucked into a corner of the French Cultural Centre"; though "decor is not the fanciest", it's "always jammed" with regulars who caution it's "cash only" while adding that it's "authentic and affordable."

	FOOD	DECOR	SERVICE	COST

Salathai Thai *Thai*

| 20 | 14 | 18 | $31 |

Downtown | 102-888 Burrard St. (bet. Robson & Smithe Sts.) | 604-683-7999

West Side | 3364 Cambie St. (bet. W. 17th & 18th Aves.) | 604-875-6999 www.salathai.ca

For "standard Thai fare", these "unpretentious" West Side and Downtown "Vancouver staples" oblige with a roster of "reliable", "reasonably priced" plates that make them "crowd-pleasers"; though some suggest the "decor's getting tired" and "service is hit-and-miss", others find "the fare more than makes up for it."

Salmon House on the Hill *Pacific NW*

| 21 | 24 | 21 | $61 |

West Vancouver | 2229 Folkestone Way (Hwy. 1, 21st St. exit) | 604-926-3212 | www.salmonhouse.com

"Million-dollar views" of "the ocean, city" and beyond bring locals and "visiting relatives" to this Pacific Northwest seafood "salmon specialist" "high above" West Vancouver, where the titular "fish is cooked over alder wood"; it can be "service-challenged" "when busy", but the authentic "Native Indian decor" makes it "like dining in a museum with the world at your feet."

Saltlik Steakhouse ❷ *Steak*

| 19 | 20 | 20 | $56 |

Downtown | 1032 Alberni St. (bet. Burrard & Thurlow Sts.) | 604-689-9749 | www.saltlik.com

"Straightforward steaks" appeal to a "wide range of tastes", drawing suits and sports fans "before the game" to this "inviting" Downtowner with "down-to-earth service"; though it's "a little pricey", the "woody decor" with a fireplace is "modern but not austere", plus it's "convenient."

Salt Tasting Room ❷ *Deli*

| 23 | 23 | 23 | $38 |

Gastown | 45 Blood Alley (bet. Abbott & Carrall Sts.) | 604-633-1912 | www.salttastingroom.com

"It's worth the dodgy walk down Blood Alley" to "put together your own wine-and-cheese plate" from the blackboard listings offered at this "crowded" moderately priced "little find" in Gastown, where a "super staff helps pick" "amazing" deli "combinations" of *fromage* and charcuterie with "flights" of *vino*; once in the "funky" "bunker", "brave" souls are "well rewarded" with a "terrific, cool room" and a "unique experience."

	FOOD	DECOR	SERVICE	COST

Saravanaa Bhavan *Indian* | 23 | 11 | 21 | $23

West Side | 955 W. Broadway (bet. Laurel & Oak Sts.) | 604-732-7700 | www.saravanaabhavan.ca

This West Sider "is as close as you can get to authentic South Indian cuisine" say vegetarians verifying there's "so much to choose from" and perhaps the "best buffet lunch bargain in town"; acolytes ask "who cares if the decor screams 'chain restaurant'" (albeit an international one) when the fare's "reliable", the service is "friendly" and "you always feel good about the bill."

Sawasdee Thai *Thai* | 22 | 14 | 19 | $30

East Side | 4250 Main St. (E. 27th Ave.) | 604-876-4030 | www.sawasdeethairestaurant.com

"Better-than-average" Thai makes this long-standing East Sider a "go-to place" for "authentically prepared" specialties including "memorable curries"; most overlook the "adequate decor" given the "knowledgeable service" and "reasonable prices."

☑ Seasons In The Park *Pacific NW* | 23 | 26 | 24 | $57

West Side | Queen Elizabeth Park | Cambie St. (W. 33rd Ave.) | 604-874-8008 | www.vancouverdine.com

Every seat has a "drop-dead view" at this "romantic" West Side "stalwart" that's rated No. 1 for Decor in the Vancouver Survey and that fans find "a joy" for its "colourful, creative", "fresh" Pacific Northwest fare served in a "beautiful setting" atop Queen Elizabeth Park; "wine prices are more than fair", service is "attentive" and those who "take out-of-town guests" to "stroll through the gardens" sigh "no wonder it's always busy."

Senova *Portuguese/Spanish* | ▽ 23 | 21 | 22 | $44

West Side | 1864 W. 57th Ave. (bet. Angus & Cypress Sts.) | 604-266-8643

"Deliciously unpretentious" Portuguese and Spanish fare "with flair" makes this West Side "neighbourhood" haunt the destination for "excellent paella" and other Iberian dishes complemented by "fantastic wine"; the "perfect flavour combinations" coming from the open kitchen are matched with "attentive service" in a long, narrow space complete with a fireplace; N.B. there was a post-Survey change of ownership.

	FOOD	DECOR	SERVICE	COST

Sha-Lin Noodle House *Chinese*

| 20 | 7 | 14 | $19 |

West Side | 548 W. Broadway (bet. Ash & Cambie Sts.) | 604-873-1816

"Watch them make the noodles" "right before your eyes" at this "entertaining" West Sider where "not your typical" Chinese fare is "fabulous, fresh" and includes "terrific steamed dumplings"; given the "tired decor" and "marginal service", it's "not a place to linger", still, it's "so affordable" that it "keeps the crowds coming."

Shanghai Chinese Bistro *Chinese*

| 22 | 14 | 21 | $36 |

Downtown | 1128 Alberni St. (bet. Bute & Thurlow Sts.) | 604-683-8222

Locals and "tourists" alike champion the "fresh dishes and elegant preparations" at this Downtown "upscale Chinese" offering "consistent", "authentic Shanghai" fare including "hand-pulled noodles" plus some of the "best dim sum around", all at moderate prices; even those who "don't expect much atmosphere" "never miss the opportunity to go."

Shiro Japanese Ⓜ *Japanese*

| 27 | 14 | 21 | $31 |

West Side | 3096 Cambie St. (W. 15th Ave.) | 604-874-0027

Raw fish fanciers "sit at the bar" and "watch the chef move gracefully" preparing "impeccably fresh", "authentic sushi" at this "tiny", "no-nonsense" West Side Japanese; so what if it's "cramped" say regulars who appreciate the "friendly staff" and insist that "at its cost", "it just doesn't get any better."

Shore Club, The Ⓢ *Seafood/Steak*

| 20 | 25 | 22 | $64 |

Downtown | 688 Dunsmuir St. (Granville St.) | 604-899-4400 | www.theshoreclub.ca

Cocktails at the "stunning bar" kick off a "special evening" at this "luxe" Downtown steakhouse and seafooder with "elegant" art deco decor that "feels like being on a cruise ship"; though wallet-watchers wince that the "pricey" fare is not especially "memorable" and service varies, all agree it's "worth checking out" "one of the loveliest settings in Vancouver."

Simply Thai *Thai*

| 23 | 18 | 21 | $32 |

Yaletown | 1211 Hamilton St. (bet. Davie & Drake Sts.) | 604-642-0123 | www.simplythairestaurant.com

"Distinct flavours" including <u>kaffir lime</u> and <u>Thai basil</u> draw surveyors to this moderately priced, "authentic" Siamese "in the heart of

Yaletown"; "cool, refreshing decor" featuring an open kitchen plus a "staff that makes you feel comfortable" and a "patio with a view of the action" add to the "appeal."

So.cial at Le Magasin *Pacific NW* | 18 | 19 | 17 | $45 |

Gastown | Le Magasin | 332 Water St. (bet. Cambie & Cordova Sts.) | 604-669-4488 | www.socialatlemagasin.com

Fans "feel cool walking into" this Gastown bistro in an "old building" (circa 1911) with "lots of character", where the "friendly staff" serves "tasty" Pacific Northwest fare beneath a silver-and-gold metal ceiling; foes who find "nothing exceptional" opt for the "cosy oyster bar downstairs" or "go mainly to the deli in the rear" for "housemade sandwiches and chips"; but all agree the "bill's not scary."

Splitz Grill *Burgers* | 19 | 11 | 14 | $20 |

East Side | 4242 Main St. (E. 27th Ave.) | 604-875-9711 | www.splitzgrill.com

See review in Whistler Directory.

Steamworks Transcontinental ☒ *Eclectic* | – | – | – | M |

Gastown | 601 W. Cordova St. (Seymour St.) | 604-678-8000 | www.thetranscontinental.com

"To escape the hustle and bustle of Gastown", surveyors suggest this "upscale bistro" where the "unbelievable surroundings" of an "elegant" former Canadian Pacific Railway station "evoke another era" through details such as arched windows and art deco gilding; in contrast, the Eclectic menu is strictly up to date, offering items from butter chicken to burgers, all at moderate prices; P.S. the original "sibling, Steamworks" Brewery, is nearby for an "after-work pint" of "amazing beer" and pub food.

NEW Stella's on Cambie ● *Eclectic* | 16 | 18 | 18 | $36 |

West Side | 3305 Cambie St. (17th Ave.) | 604-874-6900 | www.stellasbeer.com

"Already popular" and "always packed", this West Side sib of the East Side original offers an "unrivaled selection" of Belgian beers with a midpriced Eclectic menu including "steamed mussels" as a fast "favourite"; most report it's a "cut above pub" fare and give "kudos for service" in a "comfortable, modern" room that can get "really noisy."

	FOOD	DECOR	SERVICE	COST

Stella's Tap & Tapas Bar ● *Asian/Eclectic*

| 20 | 18 | 20 | $36 |

East Side | 1191 Commercial Dr. (William St.) | 604-254-2437 | www.stellasbeer.com

This Asian-Eclectic East Sider "rocks for casual fare" says the "hot, hip crowd" that gathers in the "modern European" setting for midpriced "small plates done right" served up by a "staff that knows its product"; some "return again and again" for the "laid-back atmosphere" and "divine beer selection" (including "lots of Belgian" brews) or to "hang out for hockey night"; N.B. its West Side sib just opened on Cambie.

Stepho's Souvlaki Greek Taverna ● *Greek*

| 20 | 13 | 17 | $25 |

West End | 1124 Davie St. (bet. Bute & Thurlow Sts.) | 604-683-2555

"Even in the worst weather" there's always a line-up" at the West End's "Costco of Greek" dining where "typical" taverna fare comes in "large portions" at "incredibly affordable" prices; "reservations aren't taken" (except for large parties), "service is hit-and-miss" and the "decor is nothing to brag about" – so some sniff it's "overrated", but "frugal" fans warn "beware: it's addictive."

Sun Sui Wah Seafood *Chinese/Seafood*

| 25 | 16 | 18 | $38 |

East Side | 3888 Main St. (E. 23rd Ave.) | 604-872-8822
Richmond | Alderbridge Pl. | 4940 No. 3 Rd. (bet. Alderbridge Way & Alexandra Rd.) | 604-273-8208
www.sunsuiwah.com

"Order whatever your waiter says" and "reap great rewards" advise "adventurous" advocates who venture "beyond the standards" at these top-rated Chinese seafood "emporia" on the East Side and in Richmond; forgive the "Holiday Inn banquet-room-meets-aircraft-hangar" decor and "service that varies" and focus on the "big selection" of "fresh, flavourful dim sum" (served only at lunch) and other fare that "won't set your wallet back."

Szechuan Chongqing *Chinese*

| 20 | 10 | 17 | $32 |

East Side | 2808 Commercial Dr. (E. 12th Ave.) | 604-254-7434

"Once you taste" the "authentic Sichuan entrees" "you won't care" about the "basic decor" at this East Side Chinese where the "spicy dishes with chile and garlic sauce" are the "comfort food" surveyors

FOOD DECOR SERVICE COST

remember most; even if it's "no longer in its glory days", "fast service" and "moderate prices" add to the appeal.

Takis Taverna *Greek*   ~~gay fr~~   ▽ 23 | 16 | 22 | $30

West End | 1106 Davie St. (bet. Bute & Thurlow Sts.) | 604-682-1336 | www.takistaverna.com   *"a must" in Vancouver*

"Smart locals" query why "crazy tourists" "line up" at other Hellenic haunts when you can "sneak into" this West End "favourite" for "hearty portions" of "hugely" "filling and satisfying" "classic Greek" fare; while the decor may be "nothing special", the "very welcoming" service and "value" contribute to a "calm atmosphere."

Tapastree *Pacific NW*   24 | 18 | 23 | $46

West End | 1829 Robson St. (bet. Denman & Gilford Sts.) | 604-606-4680 | www.tapastree.ca

"Herbivores and carnivores" alike find "superb nibbles" on the "consistently wonderful", "seasonally changing menu" of "interesting" Pacific Northwest "small plates" served "promptly" at this West End "hidden treasure"; although the "decor is a little dated", the "lively" (albeit "small") room makes for a "casual atmosphere", and the "price is right."

Teahouse in Stanley Park, The *Pacific NW*   23 | 25 | 23 | $54
(fka Sequoia Grill)

West End | Stanley Park | 7501 Stanley Park Dr. (Ferguson Point) | 604-669-3281 | www.vancouverdine.com

The "view of the ocean" is so "spectacular", romantics "almost forget everything else" at this "iconic" West Ender in Stanley Park offering "sophisticated" Pacific Northwest fare; the "friendly, well-trained staff" helps make this "elegant", "pricey but peaceful" room a "must for big occasions" and "perfect for Sunday brunch."

Z ToJo's ☒ *Japanese*   27 | 21 | 24 | $92

West Side | 1133 W. Broadway (bet. Alder & Spruce Sts.) | 604-872-8050 | www.tojos.com

"Bring along your adventuresome persona", "sit at the bar" and "throw yourself at the mercy" of "passionate artist"/chef-owner Hidekazu Tojo "to fully experience" the "individual service" and "exceptionally fresh", "sublime" "fruits of the ocean" in "imaginative" presentations at this Japanese "pinnacle of sushi" on the West Side; in the "almost cavernous" new location, surveyors say you're likely to "rub shoulders with movie stars, millionaires and artists" – just make sure to "have a rock star's wallet."

Tomahawk Barbecue *Diner*   21 | 19 | 19 | $22

North Vancouver | 1550 Philip Ave. (off Marine Dr.) | 604-988-2612 | www.tomahawkrestaurant.com

"Breakfast done right" featuring "fluffy pancakes", "free-range eggs" and "phenomenal bacon" plus a "big selection of burgers" made with organic beef and other diner-type fare draws families to this "friendly" North Shore "tradition" where the "coffee's always refilled" and patrons "leave feeling stuffed"; offering "history and novelty" since 1926, it boasts an impressive collection of "First Nations artwork" as part of the "bargain"; P.S. "save room for pie."

Tomato Fresh Food Café *Pacific NW*   17 | 16 | 17 | $33

West Side | 2486 Bayswater St. (B'way) | 604-874-6020 | www.tomatofreshfoodcafe.com

"Regulars who love" this "homey" West Sider say it "feels like you couldn't eat any healthier" than its Pacific Northwest "comfort food" with a focus on free-range and organic ingredients; while a few note sometimes "inattentive service", most agree the "bright setting" makes for an "unpretentious meal" giving "quality for the price."

Topanga Cafe Ⓢ *Mexican*   21 | 15 | 18 | $33

West Side | 2904 W. Fourth Ave. (bet. Bayswater & MacDonald Sts.) | 604-733-3713 | www.topangacafe.com

"Go early to avoid the line" counsel compadres who've "been going to" this "fixture on Fourth" for "fill-you-up" "California-style Mexican" fare "since it opened years ago" (in 1978); even if some say "it's nothing to get too excited about", it's "reasonably priced" and "as authentic as you can get" in these parts; N.B. framed place mats colored by customers serve as wall art.

Toshi Ⓢ Ⓜ *Japanese*   24 | 14 | 19 | $35

East Side | 181 E. 16th Ave. (bet. Main & Quebec Sts.) | 604-874-5173

Even though "the wait can be long" at this "small, popular", "friendly neighbourhood" East Sider, the "line-up" for "fantastic, fresh" Japanese seafood is "worth it"; those with patience overlook the "basic decor" and place themselves in the "masterful" "gentleman" "chef-

	FOOD	DECOR	SERVICE	COST

owner's hands" for omakase acolytes call "some of the best" "for the price" "anywhere in the city."

Trafalgar's Bistro *Eclectic* | 24 | 19 | 24 | $43 |

West Side | 2603 W. 16th Ave. (Trafalgar St.) | 604-739-0555 | www.trafalgars.com

"Ladies who lunch" and those seeking "intimate, candlelit dinners" relish this "lovely little" "quiet" "neighbourhood cafe" on the West Side for its "creative", "sophisticated" Eclectic fare that reflects the "owners' attention to detail"; "devotees" also "love the brunch", "delicious soups" and "especially" the "cornucopia" of "desserts from the bakery next door", plus "reasonable prices" and "personal service."

NEW Trattoria Italian Kitchen ● *Italian* | 22 | 20 | 21 | $43 |

West Side | 1850 W. Fourth Ave. (bet. Burrard & Cypress Sts.) | 604-732-1441 | www.trattoriakitchen.ca

It's almost "like an Italian wedding" for fans of the "hip bistro style" and "mouthwatering" "menu offering lots to choose from" at this "extremely popular" West Sider with a "buzz" that's a "more reasonably priced version of Downtown's Italian Kitchen"; the "down-home" fare is "served with pizzazz" by an "attentive staff", and even if it's "noisy", the "young crowd" "that loves to be seen" ups the "glitz and glam" quotient.

Tropika Malaysian Cuisine *SE Asian* | 20 | 15 | 17 | $31 |

Downtown | 1128 Robson St. (bet. Bute & Thurlow Sts.) | 604-737-6002
Richmond | Aberdeen Centre | 4151 Hazelbridge Way (Cambie Rd.) | 604-233-7002
West Side | 2975 Cambie St. (W. 14th Ave.) | 604-879-6002
www.tropika-canada.com

Straits shooters swear by this "quite authentic" casual mini-chain where a "good selection" of "consistent" "Malaysian and Thai plates" means diners can "try a lot and not feel broke at the end"; though some are "not crazy about the decor" and others feel the "service could be better", most warm to "solid Asian fare" "at reasonable prices."

NEW 2 Chefs & a Table *Pacific NW* | ▽ 19 | 18 | 19 | $34 |

East Side | 305 Alexander St. (Gore Ave.) | 778-233-1303 | www.twochefsandatable.com

"Fresh, filling" fare "hits home" at this "comfortable" Pacific Northwester that's a "great little lunch spot" and "worth the trek" to the East Side for its "frequently changing" dinner offerings (Wednesday–Sunday) including a "value" five-course tasting menu; even if the neighbourhood's "a bit sketchy", service is "super-friendly" and the "tiny room" is "perfect" for a "quiet evening" or even a small "party group."

Vera's Burger Shack *Burgers*

20 | 9 | 13 | $16

East Side | 1438 Commercial Dr. (bet. Grant & Kitchener Sts.) | 604-254-8372

East Side | 2922 Main St. (bet. 13th & 14th Aves.) | 604-709-8372

NEW Gastown | 213 Carrall St. (bet. Cordova & Water Sts.) | 604-568-5850

NEW North Vancouver | 1842 Lonsdale Ave. (bet. 18th & 19th Sts.) | 778-340-6328

West End | 1030 Davie St. (bet. Burrard & Thurlow Sts.) | 604-893-8372

West End | 1181 Denman St. (bet. Morton Ave. & Pendrell St.) | 604-681-5450

West Side | 1455 W. Broadway (bet. Granville & Hemlock Sts.) | 604-732-6328

West Side | 1925 Cornwall Ave. (bet. Cypress & Walnut Sts.) | 604-228-8372

West Side | 2188 Western Pkwy. (Dalhousie Rd.) | 604-221-8372

West Side | 7999 Granville St. (64th Ave.) | 604-264-8337

www.verasburgershack.com

"Bring your appetite" to these "rustic", "no-frills" "burger joints" that dispense "thick, juicy" patties "with myriad toppings"; most "don't go for" the "typical sports bar" "ambience or the service", but attest that when you want "to feel full all day", these "two-handers" are "worth both the coin and the calories."

Ⓩ Vij's *Indian* #1

28 | 22 | 25 | $54

West Side | 1480 W. 11th Ave. (bet. Granville & Hemlock Sts.) | 604-736-6664 | www.vijs.ca

Those who "dream about lamb popsicles on a regular basis" have "champion of hospitality" Vikram Vij to thank, and they've voted his "hip, vibrant" West Sider Vancouver's Most Popular for its "unequivocal", "unforgettable" "Indian fusion" "experience"; regulars revel in "inspirational", "skilful preparations" incorporating "old-world spices" and delivered with "service like a ballet", and though "no reservations" are accepted, even "waiting for a table is an art form" with "complimentary appetisers in the bar."

	FOOD	DECOR	SERVICE	COST

Vij's Rangoli *Indian*   26 | 19 | 23 | $30

West Side | 1488 W. 11th Ave. (bet. Granville & Hemlock Sts.) | 604-736-5711 | www.vijs.ca

Vijionaries who "don't have time" for the "eternal wait" next door score the "same delicious tastes" in the Indian "fast food with flair" ("but less formality") at this West Side "poor man's hit of heaven"; even though you might have to "elbow aside the ladies who lunch for a table", "attentive service" adds to the "cheerful" "cafeteria" atmosphere, and home cooks "love the option" of "fresh and frozen takeout."

NEW Voya   22 | 23 | 23 | $61
Restaurant & Lounge *Eclectic*

Downtown | Loden Hotel | 1177 Melville St. (bet. Bute & Thurlow Sts.) | 604-662-8904 | www.voyarestaurant.com

Hipsters and locals alike favour this "sexy", "cosy", new restaurant and lounge in Downtown's boutique Loden Hotel for its "delicious" Eclectic "share and single-portion plates" "created with care and consistency" plus "insanely" "terrific" cocktails; yes, it's pricey, but the "great service" and "modern twist" on '40s-style decor stoke the "happening" vibe.

Watermark on Kits Beach ◐ *Pacific NW*   16 | 24 | 17 | $50

West Side | 1305 Arbutus St. (Creelman Ave.) | 604-738-5487 | www.watermarkrestaurant.ca

Surveyors feel like they're "on vacation" at this West Side Pacific Northwester "right on Kits Beach" that boasts "one of the best views in Vancouver" plus "terrific" "people-watching"; those who come for "gorgeous sunsets" "aren't too concerned" about "so-so" fare that "could use a bit of work", and considering the "waiters try hard", most are "grateful for the reasonable prices."

Water St. Café *Italian/Pacific NW*   19 | 18 | 20 | $41

Gastown | 300 Water St. (Cambie St.) | 604-689-2832

"Roaming tourists in search of sustenance" or "dinner before the show" flock to this Gastown Italian–Pacific Northwester for an "enjoyable meal" of "solid fare" in "quaint surroundings" "right in front of the Steam Clock"; service is "adequate" – some even call it "brusque" – but there are "no complaints" over its "reasonable prices" and appeal "for lunch."

	FOOD	DECOR	SERVICE	COST

☑ West *Pacific NW* 27 | 24 | 26 | $88

West Side | 2881 Granville St. (W. 13th Ave.) | 604-738-8938 |
www.westrestaurant.com

"Those who love exciting" cuisine "can't wait to go back" for chef Warren Geraghty's "imaginative", "perfectly prepared and artfully presented" seasonal Pacific Northwest plates at this "lively, congenial and sophisticated" West Sider that's a "tour de force" serving "heaven in every bite"; delivering a "full package" of "impeccable service", "incredible tasting menus" and "superb" vintages from a "must-see wall of wine", it's naturally "not inexpensive", but is "worth it" for a "truly fabulous" "night to remember."

Wild Garlic Bistro *Pacific NW* 24 | 16 | 24 | $41

West End | 792 Denman St. (bet. Alberni & Robson Sts.) | 604-687-1663 |
www.wildgarlicbistro.com

"You have to love garlic" agree acolytes of this "warm" West End "neighbourhood" "hideaway" whose "kitchen cranks out consistently delicious" Pacific Northwest fare much of which features the fragrant bulb; even if "it's not much to look at inside", this "small, cosy" haunt attracts "colourful locals" with its "congenial service" and 40 different martinis.

Wild Rice *Chinese* 23 | 21 | 20 | $39

Downtown | 117 W. Pender St. (bet. Abbott & Cambie Sts.) | 604-642-2882 |
www.wildricevancouver.com

For a "change of Asian pace", regulars return to this midpriced Downtown "chic and tasty" "favourite" for "innovative" "Chinese-style tapas" of "East-West fusion delicately done"; though some suggest "it helps if you're wafer-thin and thirtysomething", this "cool", "modern" serving of "yin and yang" with spotty service is "still sexy" in its setting that's "more like a living room."

William Tell Restaurant, The Ⓜ *Swiss* 22 | 21 | 23 | $65

Downtown | Georgian Court Hotel | 765 Beatty St. (bet. Robson & W. Georgia Sts.) | 604-688-3504 | www.thewmtell.com

"Elegant dining never goes out of style" at this "high-end" Downtown "classic" for "solid, elegant" Swiss, French and Pacific Northwest cuisine with "everything done well" in a "beautiful, romantic" hotel setting "reminiscent of Europe"; while style mavens call the "country-club atmosphere" "stuffy", others enjoy the "relaxed yet formal sur-roundings" and "professional service"; P.S. try the "casual room out front for lunch."

Yew Restaurant & Bar   *Pacific NW*

22 | 25 | 24 | $63

Downtown | Four Seasons | 791 W. Georgia St. (bet. Granville & Howe Sts.) | 604-689-9333 | www.fourseasons.com/vancouver

Everyone from "power-lunchers" to "distracted gawkers" ("who just walked in?") frequents this "inspired" Pacific Northwest "oasis of fine dining" with "great buzz" and a 40-ft. ceiling Downtown in the "swank" Four Seasons hotel; from "decadent mac 'n' cheese with truf-fles" to "magic", "never-intrusive service" and a "communal table made from one huge tree", it "accommodates anything you want" – except perhaps a small tab.

Victoria & Vancouver Island

Aerie Resort
Dining Room, The   *French/Pacific NW*

25 | 24 | 25 | $77

Malahat | Aerie Resort | 600 Ebedora Ln. (Spectacle Lake turnoff) | 250-743-7115 | www.aerie.bc.ca

"It's hard to imagine a more breathtaking setting" marvel admirers of this "first-rate resort" near the Malahat summit where the French–Pacific Northwest cuisine is "stellar and the view nearly tops it"; those who "make the trip" report "excellence all-around" thanks to "local ingredients" and "exceptional service", adding that even if "it isn't cheap", it's "perfect for a spa weekend" and "as ro-mantic as it gets."

Amusé Bistro   Ⓜ *French*

23 | 18 | 21 | $49

Shawnigan Lake | 1753 Shawnigan-Mill Bay Rd. (Wallbank Rd.) | 250-743-3667 | www.amusebistro.com

Gastronauts who detour to rural Shawnigan Lake, between Victoria and Duncan, alight at Bradford Boisvert's intimate French "hidden gem" in an "enchanting location"; locavores who insist "this is what the 100-mile diet was meant to be" salute the "incredible chef" for such "creative" "dining at a high level" and "affordable price" and reckon "this place kicks butt on fancy urban restaurants."

	FOOD	DECOR	SERVICE	COST

🆕 Aura *Pacific NW* — 24 | 22 | 23 | $53

Downtown | The Inn at Laurel Point | 680 Montreal St. (Belleville St.) | Victoria | 250-386-8721 | www.aurarestaurant.ca

Visitors and locals get "unbeatable views" along with the "inventive" Pacific Northwest cuisine with Pacific Rim influences (including "succulent steaks and chops") and "terrific service" at this Downtowner "set right on the harbour" at the Laurel Point Inn; even if doubters dub it "just so-so", most find it "excellent all-around" and "priced fairly" – "especially for a hotel."

🆕 Bard & Banker Public House *Pub food* — 18 | 23 | 18 | $31

Downtown | 1022 Government St. (Fort St.) | Victoria | 250-953-9993 | www.bardandbanker.com

"It feels like Britain" say "tourists and locals alike" at this Downtowner, which delivers "perfectly acceptable", midpriced pub fare in an "impressive" "restoration of an old bank"; with "lots of nooks" and an "excellent selection of beers" (30 on tap), "it's fine for the basics", and even if "service can be slow", servers "have a keen eye for almost-empty pints"; N.B. the "house rocks with live local music" nightly.

Blue Crab Bar & Grill, The *Seafood* — 23 | 22 | 22 | $53

Downtown | Coast Victoria Harbourside Hotel & Marina | 146 Kingston St. (Montreal St., waterfront) | Victoria | 250-480-1999 | www.bluecrab.ca

"What's not to love" about "delicious seafood at satisfactory prices" in a "great location overlooking the harbour" ask finny fans of this Downtowner in the Coast Victoria Harbourside Hotel; while "service is uneven", most "would certainly go back" for "solid fare" including "excellent" crab cakes or for "drinks after work" plus "knockout views of the water."

Blue Fox Cafe, The *Eclectic* — 22 | 15 | 20 | $21

Downtown | 101-919 Fort St. (Quadra St.) | Victoria | 250-380-1683

"Victorians get up early for breakfast" at this Eclectic Downtown "legend" that delivers "huge portions" of "wonderful eggs Benedict" and other "innovative dishes" made with "fresh ingredients"; even if it's "elbow-room slim" and the "line-up" (especially on weekends) is "out the door", those craving "morning-after food", be it "organic or greasy", and who "don't mind the bustle" swear it'll "start your day off right."

	FOOD	DECOR	SERVICE	COST

☑ Brasserie L'Ecole 🔁Ⓜ *French* `27` `23` `26` `$50`
Downtown | 1715 Government St. (bet. Fisgard & Herald Sts.) | Victoria | 250-475-6260 | www.lecole.ca

For a "truly French feel" "in Anglophone Victoria", this "unpretentious" "classic bistro" Downtown "favourite" has Francophiles almost "lost for words" over its "beyond-superb steaks" and "top-notch frites"; add in "amazing" wines ferried by "a knowledgeable staff" and most "would definitely eat here again"; N.B. a post-Survey renovation is not reflected in the Decor score.

Cafe Brio *Pacific NW* `26` `23` `25` `$53`
Downtown | 944 Fort St. (bet. Quadra & Vancouver Sts.) | Victoria | 250-383-0009 | www.cafe-brio.com

Patrons "feel like part of the family" at this casual Downtown "oldie but goodie" in a Tuscan-style setting that's a "neighbourhood" "treasure" where the Pacific Northwest "food is an art form" and the "friendly owners" oversee "staffers who love what they do"; fans citing a "long wine list" with some "rare bottles" and "waiters who can't do enough to help" say it's "expensive but worth it", insisting "you can't go wrong."

Camille's 🔁Ⓜ *Pacific NW* `27` `23` `26` `$52`
Downtown | 45 Bastion Sq. (Langley St.) | Victoria | 250-381-3433 | www.camillesrestaurant.com

It's a "can't-miss meal" say surveyors who've sampled the "exceptional" Pacific Northwest fare at this "romantic", "cosy warren of rooms" Downtown, where the menu of "superbly cooked, fresh" fare "changes frequently"; the "consistent quality", "wonderful service" and "incredibly fair prices" all add up to a "guaranteed pleasure" worthy of a "special occasion."

Deep Cove Chalet Ⓜ *French* `26` `22` `24` `$74`
Sidney | 11190 Chalet Rd. (Tatlow Rd.) | 250-656-3541 | www.deepcovechalet.com

Gourmets gravitate to the "divine", "high-end French cuisine" and "remarkable cellar" at Sidney's "off-the-beaten-track" "cute little cottage on the water" in Deep Cove, where "charming", "old-school" chef-owner Pierre Koffel "makes sure you're taken care of"; add in "smooth, professional service" for an "experience" patrons assure is "worth the cost."

NEW Edge Restaurant, The Ⓢ Ⓜ *Pacific NW* | - | - | - | E |

Sooke | 6688 Sooke Rd. (Otter Point Rd.) | 778-425-3343 | www.edgerestaurant.ca

Former long-time Sooke Harbour House executive chef Edward Tuson and partner Gemma Claridge (hence Ed-ge) recently opened to wide acclaim their affordable, casual Pacific Northwest bistro in Downtown Sooke; almost everything served in the richly coloured, warm, onetime fish 'n' chips shop is prepared in-house, including homemade sausages, desserts and pasta, with plenty of ingredients foraged right from the neighbourhood.

Ⓩ Empress Room *Pacific NW* | 23 | 28 | 25 | VE |

Downtown | The Fairmont Empress | 721 Government St. (bet. Belleville & Humboldt Sts.) | Victoria | 250-389-2727 | www.fairmont.com

For a "grand old British dining experience", this "pricey, lovely" "Victorian gem" in the heart of Downtown at the Fairmont Empress – rated No. 1 for Decor in Vancouver Island – makes for a "wonderful night" of "fantastic service" and "fabulous" Pacific Northwest fare; "drop by the Bengal Lounge for a martini" beforehand to complete an "over-the-top" evening that's "worth every penny" for those who "want to feel like royalty."

Ferris' Oyster Bar & Grill *Seafood* | 22 | 17 | 20 | $34 |

Downtown | 536 Yates St. (bet. Government & Wharf Sts.) | Victoria | 250-360-1824 | www.ferrisoysterbar.com

"If you love oysters" and "enormous burgers", this "casual", "funky, cool" seafooder "located in an older building Downtown" is known for "moderately priced", "fresh, creative" "drinks and comfort food"; "locals keep coming back" for "pleasant, attentive service" and report the "low-key upstairs" bar will especially "blow your socks off" for cocktails and "appies."

Haro's Restaurant & Bar *Pacific NW* | ▽ 20 | 21 | 20 | $58 |

Sidney | Sidney Pier Hotel & Spa | 9805 Seaport Pl. (Beacon Ave.) | 250-655-9445 | www.sidneypier.com

Upscale casual dining on Sidney's waterfront comes with vistas across to Mount Baker at this pricey, fireplace-adorned Pacific Northwest newcomer in the Sidney Pier Hotel & Spa, equidistant between BC Ferries Swartz Bay terminal and Victoria; menus focus on local meats, Ocean

Wise seafood and housemade pastas, offered with an extensive BC wine list, while a summertime draw is the heated outdoor oceanside terrace.

Ⓩ Hastings House *Pacific NW* | 27 | 26 | 28 | $93 |

Salt Spring Island | Hastings House Country House Hotel | 160 Upper Ganges Rd. (bet. Churchill & Lower Ganges Rd.) | 250-537-2362 | www.hastingshouse.com

"All dining experiences should be this wonderful" gush guests at this seasonal (mid-March to mid-November) Pacific Northwest "treasure" with a "considerate" staff (rated No. 1 for Service in and around Vancouver Island) on an "elegant country estate" that's a "must" on Salt Spring"; the "meal to remember" comes complete with "astonishing" fare featuring "lots of local ingredients" and a backdrop of "lovely water views", leaving smitten surveyors sighing it's "expensive", but also "as attractive as it gets."

Il Terrazzo *Italian* | 24 | 23 | 22 | $53 |

Downtown | 555 Johnson St. (bet. Government & Wharf Sts.) | Victoria | 250-361-0028 | www.ilterrazzo.com

Fans say "you can't go wrong" at this "busy", "well-hidden" Downtown "icon" "in Old Town Victoria", where "delicious" Italian fare is served by a "helpful staff" amid a "beautiful ambience" of "cosy candlelight" and six fireplaces; some choose the "outside covered patio" as "the place to be year-round" to "take a date" or just for a "fabulous evening."

J & J Wonton Noodle House Ⓢ Ⓜ *Chinese* | 24 | 12 | 18 | $23 |

Downtown | 1012 Fort St. (bet. Cook & Vancouver Sts.) | Victoria | 250-383-0680 | www.jjnoodlehouse.com

Surveyors are "never disappointed" with the "fast, tasty" and budget-friendly "noodles made on-site" at this Downtown Victoria "basic room" that's an "institution" for the "Chinese equivalent of home-style" fare; those who "like it, love it" despite the "noisy, fluorescent-cafeteria" digs, though some "just wish they delivered."

Ⓩ Keg Steakhouse & Bar *Steak* | 20 | 17 | 19 | $47 |

Downtown | 500 Fort St. (Wharf St.) | Victoria | 250-386-7789
Saanich | 3940 Quadra St. (bet. Hulford St. & Reynolds Rd.) | Victoria | 250-479-1651
www.kegsteakhouse.com
See review in Vancouver Directory.

	FOOD	DECOR	SERVICE	COST

Lure *Seafood*

| | 24 | 23 | 22 | $59 |

Downtown | Delta Victoria Ocean Pointe Resort & Spa | 45 Songhees Rd. (Kimta Rd.) | Victoria | 250-360-5873 | www.lurevictoria.com

Fin fanatics find "fresh, delicious seafood" "perfectly cooked and exquisitely presented" at this "sleek, modern" upscale-casual room Downtown in the Delta Victoria Ocean Pointe Resort & Spa that boasts "spectacular views" of the "inner harbour" through walls of windows; service that's "attentive but not overbearing" adds to the allure.

Marina Restaurant *Pacific NW/Seafood*

| | 21 | 23 | 21 | $50 |

Oak Bay | 1327 Beach Dr. (bet. Currie & Windsor Rds.) | Victoria | 250-598-8555 | www.marinarestaurant.com

"Come for the sunset" and "beautiful ocean view all-round" say those who "make the short drive from Downtown" to Oak Bay for "fine" fare at this Pacific Northwest-seafooder with "professional service"; "decor is luxurious" and the "price is right", plus the "outside deck is awesome in summer."

Pagliacci's *Italian*

| | 21 | 18 | 19 | $31 |

Downtown | 1011 Broad St. (bet. Broughton & Fort Sts.) | Victoria | 250-386-1662 | www.pagliaccis.ca

A "must-visit" Downtown "classic" if only for "cheesecake that's worth every calorie", this "quirky", "unbeatable-for-value" Italian is "like a little bit of NYC in Victoria"; despite "tables so close you can kiss your neighbour", "variable service" and sniffs that "it's over-rated", most find it "well worth the wait" in the "line to get in"; N.B. there's live music often.

⚡ Panache *Pacific NW*

| | 28 | 26 | 27 | $73 |

Langford | Westin Bear Mtn. | 1999 Country Club Way (Bear Mountain Pkwy.) | 250-391-7160 | www.bearmountain.ca

Scratch golfers and duffers report "some of the best fine dining in Victoria" enhanced by a "superb wine list" at this "innovative", upscale-casual Pacific Northwesterner – rated No. 1 for Food in and around Vancouver Island – overlooking Langford's "scenic" Westin Bear Mountain Golf Resort; handicappers heartily hail chef Iain Rennie for "fresh, simple dishes well done" and shrug even if "it is expensive", "it's worth it."

	FOOD	DECOR	SERVICE	COST

Paprika Bistro 🍽️Ⓜ️ *French/Italian*   27 | 23 | 25 | $64

Oak Bay | 2524 Estevan Ave. (bet. Dunlevy Rd. & Musgrave St.) | Victoria | 250-592-7424 | www.paprika-bistro.com

Those seeking "delicious" French and Italian dishes head "out of the way" to this "favourite" Oak Bay "neighbourhood" "jewel" with "upscale" fare and "friendly, informative" service; although "a bit hard to find", most agree the "organic goodies" and "excellent wines" are "worth the search" and (even if you want "to get engaged") this "romantic gem" is "one of the best."

Pescatore's   20 | 18 | 21 | $53
Seafood & Grill *Pacific NW/Seafood*

Downtown | 614 Humboldt St. (bet. Gordon & Government Sts.) | Victoria | 250-385-4512 | www.pescatores.com

"If you want fish" or "lovely oysters" with an "excellent", "unoaked BC Chardonnay", this "dependable" Pacific Northwest seafood specialist situated near the "scenic inner harbour" might as well be "your first stop" in Downtown Victoria; friends "love" "the cool", "old-fashioned ceiling fans" and fare that's even "better than the decor" and applaud "quick, friendly service."

🆕 Pizzeria Prima Strada *Pizza*   21 | 17 | 19 | $24

Downtown | 105-230 Cook St. (bet. Oliphant Ave. & Oxford St.) | Victoria | 250-590-8595 | www.pizzeriaprimastrada.com

"It's like being transported back to Italy" for "thin-crust" aficionados at this Downtown Italian where "mouthwatering", "wood-fired" pizza that "tastes like Naples" is brought by an "unpretentious", "attentive staff"; pie purists "love the quality" and the "focus on local ingredients", but "just wish it could seat more people" since it's "always busy."

Pointe Restaurant at   25 | 27 | 24 | $91
Wickaninnish Inn, The *Pacific NW*

Tofino | Wickaninnish Inn | 500 Osprey Ln. (Lynn Rd.) | 250-725-3106 | www.wickinn.com

Stormchasers who "watch the waves crash on the rocks" at this "most romantic spot" in Tofino's Wickaninnish Inn "love the view" as well as the "awesome" Pacific Northwest "dining experience" that comes from "ambitious sourcing" of "superb ingredients right from the sea"; though a few doubters find the service not quite as "spectacular" "as the location", most marvel it's "amazing in all respects", adding that's "as it should be for the price."

Rebar Modern Food *Eclectic/Vegetarian*   25 | 18 | 19 | $26

Downtown | 50 Bastion Sq. (Langley St.) | Victoria | 250-361-9223 | www.rebarmodernfood.com

"Even non-vegetarians will be in heaven" aver acolytes of the "innovative, healthy" midpriced fare at this "hip", "high-energy" Eclectic-vegetarian Downtown that "does everything well" from "stellar salads" to "sumptuous desserts"; even "borderline carnivores" confess the "almond burger will convert the most devout sceptics" in this "colourful", "eccentric" setting.

Red Fish Blue Fish *Seafood*   25 | 16 | 18 | $16

Downtown | Brough Street Pier | 1006 Wharf St. (Broughton St.) | Victoria | 250-298-6877 | www.redfish-bluefish.com

"Word is out and the line-ups are long" for the "best seafood you'll get from" a "cargo container converted" into a "stand on the docks" say finny fans of this "Ocean Wise" "bare-bones" Downtowner; even if there are "no tables, just benches", its "new take on classic fish 'n' chips" and "tacos second to none" are "good for your taste buds and conscience" – and also your wallet.

Restaurant Matisse Ⓜ *French*   26 | 22 | 27 | $63

Downtown | 512 Yates St. (Wharf St.) | Victoria | 250-480-0883 | www.restaurantmatisse.com

"Exceptional French cuisine" lures Francophiles to this "cosy" Downtown "petite restaurant offering a grand dining experience" complete with "attentive", "friendly service" that fans call "close to perfect"; "fresh, local, organic" fare in a setting complete with white tablecloths and flowers make it "top-drawer all the way" and "worth every penny."

Siam Thai *Thai*   21 | 13 | 19 | $24

Downtown | 512 Fort St. (bet. Langley & Wharf Sts.) | Victoria | 250-383-9911

Spice hounds hail this Downtowner as "one of Victoria's oldest and best" for "flavourful" Thai dishes including "incredible" pad Thai and curries; even if the decor is a little "bland", given the friendly prices and service, "you won't be disappointed."

Smoken Bones *BBQ/Creole*

23 | 13 | 20 | $27

Langford | 101-721 Station Ave. (bet. Meaford Ave. & Millstream Rd.) | 250-391-6328 | www.smokenbones.ca

Better "wear elastic-waist pants" to accommodate the "huge portions" of "awesome" Southern fare at this affordable, "unpretentious" Langford smokehouse offering "fall-off-the-bone" ribs, pulled pork and other BBQ "delights" plus Creole specialties; true, the decor is "not the most stylish", but "it doesn't have to be" given the "decent service" and "focus on local" ingredients."

☒ Sobo *Eclectic*

27 | 16 | 18 | $36

Tofino | Conradi Bldg. | 311 Neill St. (bet. 1st & 2nd Sts.) | 250-725-2341 | www.sobo.ca

At this Eclectic (the name's short for Sophisticated Bohemian) that's moved to larger quarters in Tofino, chef-owner Lisa Ahier "has a magic touch" with "wonderful, inventive" seafood and other dishes featuring "locally sourced ingredients" say followers who'd "travel hours for her chowders"; "be ready to wait" for "generous servings" of "unpretentious" fare that "excites" at "exceptional value."

☒ Sooke Harbour House *Pacific NW*

27 | 26 | 26 | $86

Sooke | Sooke Harbour House | 1528 Whiffen Spit Rd. (Hwy. 14) | 250-642-3421 | www.sookeharbourhouse.com

With its "inspired and obsessively local" Pacific Northwest cuisine of "fresh, seasonal" ingredients "often grown right on the property", Sinclair and Frederique Philip's "outstanding" "long-time destination favourite" "right on the water" in Sooke "never fails to impress" with "tasteful attention to every detail"; an "eloquent staff" helps navigate an extensive wine cellar that's "among the region's best" at this "understated" room that yields a "total country-inn experience."

Stage ◑ *Mediterranean*

26 | 23 | 22 | $44

Downtown | 1307 Gladstone Ave. (Fernwood Rd.) | Victoria | 250-388-4222 | www.stagewinebar.com

"Lots of hard choices" are presented by the "appealing menu" at this "amazing wine bar" in a "hip hood" Downtown in Victoria where "tasty" Med small plates are served "by a knowledgeable staff"; though it's "a bit pricey", "many nice BC wines by the glass" help make it a "hit on all fronts", especially "before a show at the Belfry" nearby.

| | FOOD | DECOR | SERVICE | COST |

Temple ●🖪 *Pacific NW*

21 | 21 | 21 | $44

Downtown | 525 Fort St. (Langley St.) | Victoria | 250-383-2313 |
www.thetemple.ca

"On weekends", expect congregations of "the young and the beautiful"
at this Downtown "favourite", where a "super-cool", "modern interior" is
the backdrop for "clever martinis" and "organic-when-possible"
Pacific Northwest fare; though a few grouse it's "too trendy" and
"slightly overpriced", believers assembling for "late drinks and
snacks" chant "we need more" like it.

Zambri's 🖪🅼 *Italian*

26 | 16 | 23 | $44

Downtown | 110-911 Yates St. (bet. Quadra & Vancouver Sts.) | Victoria |
250-360-1171 | www.zambris.ca

"Fresh, local" ingredients "are left to speak for themselves" at chef-
owner Peter Zambri's "busy" Downtown trattoria offering "vibrant
pastas", a "handful of entrees" and "delicious vegetable sides";
"value-priced wines" for pairing are "recommended by an educated
staff" amid "Italian farmhouse decor" for an experience so "charming"
"you'll forget you're in a strip mall."

Whistler

🆉 Araxi *Pacific NW*

26 | 23 | 25 | $75

Whistler | 4222 Village Sq. (Whistler Way) | 604-932-4540 |
www.araxi.com

"Chef James Walt is attached at the hip to local farmers, ranchers and
fisherfolk" so it's no surprise that the "divine", "imaginative" fare at
this pricey Pacific Northwester features "fresh produce sourced within
100 miles" of Whistler Village; "highly competent" service in the
"beautifully elegant room" gives a "big-night-out buzz", whether
you're at the "cool outdoor bar with your boots on" or indoors keeping
"an eye out for celebrities."

Aubergine Grille *Pacific NW*

24 | 19 | 21 | $48

Whistler | Westin Resort & Spa | 4090 Whistler Way (base of Whistler Mtn.) |
604-935-4344 | www.westin.com

"Hidden away" in the Village on a "pathway to other places", this
Westin-based Pacific Northwester offers intrepid explorers "delightful"
"reasonably priced" fare brought by an "attentive", "always smiling"

staff; the "beautiful", "relaxing" atmosphere at the base of Whistler Mountain also makes it a "favourite breakfast buffet" for early-risers.

☑ Bear Foot Bistro *Pacific NW*

27 | 22 | 26 | $76

Whistler | Listel Whistler Hotel | 4121 Village Green (Whistler Way) | 604-932-3433 | www.bearfootbistro.com

"Hedonists" "forget about skiing in heaven" in favor of this "over-the-top experience" in the Village's Listel Hotel that's rated No. 1 for Food and Service in Whistler, where "exquisitely creative" Pacific Northwest cuisine from a kitchen "insanely committed to flavour" meets "flawless service" and the "deepest" "legendary wine cellar" in a "romantic" room; "if you're looking for a party, roll up to the champagne bar" – either way, cognoscenti quip "you'll leave barefoot after paying the bill."

Caramba! Restaurante *Mediterranean*

18 | 17 | 19 | $40

Whistler | 12-4314 Main St. (bet. Northlands & Village Gate Blvds.) | 604-938-1879 | www.caramba-restaurante.com

"Quick service" and mounds of "tasty" "eclectic" Mediterranean fare "washed down with sangria" make this "reasonably priced" Whistler Village mainstay a "local favourite"; despite the "wood-burning oven", the decor reads a little "tired", but it's still a "family place" that's "great for kids" – though you may wish to "bring earplugs."

☑ Edgewater Lodge *Continental/Pacific NW*

23 | 24 | 23 | $52

Whistler | Green Lake | 8020 Alpine Way (Hwy. 99) | 604-932-0688 | www.edgewater-lodge.com

"You can't beat the setting and the view" for a "quiet meal" at this "peaceful, serene" Continental-PacificNorthwester – rated No. 1 for Decor in Whistler – with a "spectacular location" on Green Lake; "solid culinary skills" come through in "classic dishes" (e.g. seared duck breast and venison medallions), and "excellent service" assures "peace of mind" for the harried; N.B. closed to the public for the 2010 Olympics, it reopens to all April 30, 2010.

Elements Urban Tapas Parlour *Eclectic*

25 | 20 | 21 | $37

Whistler | Summit Lodge | 4359 Main St. (Northlands Blvd.) | 604-932-5569 | www.wildwoodrestaurants.ca

Perhaps "Whistler's best-kept secret", this midpriced Eclectic tapas bar "just on the outskirts of the Village" has "cornered the market" for "small plates" (a "change from normal ski fare") with "many tasty options"; "subtle, yet attentive service" in a setting featuring suede banquettes and copper accents contributes to a "calming atmosphere", and fans declare brunch "brilliant."

Fifty Two 80 Bistro *Pacific NW*   22 | 22 | 23 | $65

Whistler | Four Seasons Resort Whistler | 4591 Blackcomb Way (Lorimer Rd.) | 604-935-3400 | www.fourseasons.com

"Service and service" is how surveyors sum up this "excellent-value" Upper Village bistro in the Four Seasons Resort Whistler where the "professional, friendly and very knowledgeable" staff delivers "inventive" but not "fussy" Pacific Northwest fare; "outside by the pond on a warm day" is especially "soothing" to some, while others "love the bar" and "stunning decor" indoors that features sleek wood and an open fireplace.

⚡ Hy's Steakhouse *Steak*   23 | 22 | 24 | $78

Whistler | Delta Whistler Village Suites | 4308 Main St. (Northlands Blvd.) | 604-905-5555 | www.hyssteakhouse.com

"After a long day on the mountain", this "classic" Whistler Village steakhouse (a sib to Vancouver's Hy's Encore) "is the place" for "outstanding Western beef" counsel carnivores captivated by "delicious" cuts, "killer cheese bread" and "Caesar salad made tableside"; the "warm, wood-paneled" room is "always crowded" and the price "high", but an "attentive staff" that seems to "genuinely enjoy being there" and an "extensive wine list" are as comforting as "sitting by the fire."

Il Caminetto di Umberto *Italian*   24 | 22 | 24 | $71

Whistler | 4242 Village Stroll (Whistler Village Sq.) | 604-932-4442 | www.umberto.com/village.htm

"Simply wonderful" Italian right "in the heart of the Village" in Whistler draws fans to this pricey trattoria where "thoughtfully prepared" plates of "delicious" Tuscan fare arrive via owner Umberto Menghi's "attentive staff"; the terra-cotta walled room is "meant for people-watching", and there's also a new piano bar plus an expanded patio "for an amazing meal outside."

⚡ Keg Steakhouse & Bar *Steak*   20 | 17 | 19 | $47

Whistler | Whistler Village Inn | 4429 Sundial Pl. (off Blackcomb Way) | 604-932-5151 | www.kegsteakhouse.com

See review in Vancouver Directory.

	FOOD	DECOR	SERVICE	COST

☒ La Rua Restaurante *Pacific NW*

25 | **22** | **23** | **$72**

Whistler | Le Chamois | 4557 Blackcomb Way (bet. Glacier Dr. & Lorimer Rd.) | 604-932-5011 | www.larua-restaurante.com

A "large" and "varied menu" of "consistently exceptional" Pacific Northwest fare – including "amazing pasta" and "wonderful game in winter" – draws diners to this "delightful" rustic Upper Village space in Whistler's Le Chamois hotel; while it may not be "as flashy or high-profile" as other spots, regulars report that "excellent" service from the "friendly staff" and "value" for the area make it rate return visits.

Monk's Grill *Eclectic*

18 | **19** | **18** | **$54**

Whistler | 4555 Blackcomb Way (Lorimer Rd.) | 604-932-9677 | www.monksgrill.com

Slopesters looking to add a "buzz" to their "après ski" slide into this casual Whistler Village Eclectic for its "wonderful view and location" (right at the base of Blackcomb Mountain); with fare that's "just ok", some prefer to go for "drinks and appetizers" or even just "nachos and beer" and "watch the world go by."

Mountain Club Restaurant & Lounge, The ❶ *Pacific NW*

21 | **22** | **20** | **$58**

Whistler | 40-4314 Main St. (Northlands Blvd.) | 604-932-6009 | www.themountainclub.ca

Dinner "gets off to a fine start" with a martini served up by an "excellent bartender" confirms the cocktail crowd that clamours for this "unique" Pacific Northwest Whistler Village sibling to Vancouver's Ocean Club; the "exciting", "surprisingly comforting" fare offered on a "not large" but "varied" menu, coupled with an "extensive wine list" plus "upscale lodge" decor all contribute to the "clubby" "atmosphere."

Quattro at Whistler ☒ *Italian*

23 | **21** | **23** | **$64**

Whistler | Pinnacle International Hotel | 4319 Main St. (Northlands Blvd.) | 604-905-4844 | www.quattrorestaurants.com

Sated schussers say the "outstanding" "old-style Italian" dishes provide an "incredible (and filling) experience" at this "beautiful, contemporary room" "removed from the hustle and bustle of Whistler Village" in the Pinnacle International Hotel; "good prices" and an "accommodating staff" "willing to modify dishes to customers' tastes" complete the "fitting end to a day on the slopes."

☒ Rim Rock Cafe *Pacific NW/Seafood*   26 | 23 | 25 | $66

Whistler | 2117 Whistler Rd. (Hwy. 99) | 604-932-5565 | www.rimrockwhistler.com

The "fantastic" Pacific Northwest fare and seafood is so "beautifully prepared" at this "pretty", pricey Whistler creekside "old-time favourite" that dishes like the "exceptional caribou" seduce even those who "don't normally like game"; the "atmosphere is mountain comfort", particularly when "sitting by one of the two fireplaces" and savouring the "excellent wine" or "selection of craft brews", all delivered with "outstanding service."

Splitz Grill *Burgers*   19 | 11 | 14 | $20

Whistler | 104-4369 Main St. (Northlands Blvd.) | 604-938-9300 | www.splitzgrill.com

"Sign me up" for "freshly grilled" "hamburgers with 20 topping options" root chowhound cheerleaders of this "family-friendly" Whistler burger bar; as "nothing is pre-fab", you "create your own" "cheap, easy" meal, but it's best to "go early to avoid line-ups"; N.B. the original location is under new ownership and the original owners now run the new Vancouver outpost.

Sushi Village *Japanese*   23 | 13 | 18 | $41

Whistler | 4272 Mountain Sq. (Whistler Village Sq.) | 604-932-3330 | www.sushivillage.com

"Superb rice" plus "fresh" ingredients add up to "sushi paradise" at this long-standing Village Japanese where the "padded seats are as comfy" as the menu is "solid"; decor might be a little "dated", but it's made up for by "prompt, friendly service" and prices that "hit the spot"; just "get there before 6 PM" advise afishionados, "or you'll be waiting awhile."

Trattoria di Umberto *Italian*   24 | 22 | 22 | $60

Whistler | Mountainside Lodge | 4417 Sundial Pl. (Whistler Village Sq.) | 604-932-5858 | www.hotelvilladelia.com

"Wonderful" Italian fare including "specials that can knock your socks off" attracts *amici* to Umberto Menghi's Village Square trattoria where the "open kitchen" turns dinner into "entertainment"; though service can be "rushed" when the "frenetic Tuscan room" is "packed with the *après* 'in' crowd", the "upbeat staff makes the experience worth the price."

Wildflower, The *Pacific NW* | 22 | 22 | 22 | $64 |

Whistler | Chateau Whistler Resort | 4599 Chateau Blvd. (Blackcomb Way) | 604-938-2033 | www.fairmont.com

"Unbeatable views" from its "mountainside location" make this "pretty", pricey Upper Village Pacific Northwester in the Chateau Whistler Resort "a bit of an oasis in the crazy excitement" of the town say "happy skiers" who "can't imagine a better place" for a "lovely Sunday brunch"; the fine "Fairmont Hotels service" and a "menu that satisfies both casual and high-end diners" complete the picture.

NIGHTLIFE
DIRECTORY

Nightlife

Ratings & Symbols

Appeal, Decor and **Service** are rated on the Zagat 0 to 30 scale.

Cost reflects our surveyors' estimated price (in Canadian dollars) of a typical single drink. For places listed without ratings, the price range is shown as follows:

⌐ᴵ	below $5	ᴱ	$9 to $11
ᴹ	$5 to $8	ⱽᴱ	$12 or above

Vancouver

MOST POPULAR

1. Opus Bar
2. Commodore Ballrm.
3. Bacchus Lounge
4. Celebrities
5. Shark Club

TOP APPEAL

- 26 Commodore Ballrm.
  Bacchus Lounge
- 24 Railway Club
- 23 Opus Bar
- 21 Ginger Sixty Two

AuBAR Nightclub

18 | 18 | 19 | $9

Downtown | 674 Seymour St. (bet. Dunsmuir & Georgia Sts.) | 604-648-2227 | www.aubarnightclub.com

"Beautiful people" head to this "trendy" club Downtown to dance to DJ-spun hip-hop, R&B and reggae; a "friendly staff" caters to an "upbeat" "professional crowd" that "loves the nightlife"; but a few barflies flit on by, griping "there's always a wait" to party among the "pretentious."

⊿ Bacchus Lounge

26 | 26 | 23 | $12

Downtown | Wedgewood Hotel | 845 Hornby St. (bet. Robson & Smithe Sts.) | 604-608-5319 | www.wedgewoodhotel.com

"As many wedding rings slip on as off" at this "plush" lounge in the Wedgewood Hotel that fans agree is the "classiest in town"; everyone from "Downtown business types" to "tony" "thirty- and fortysomethings" likes the "fantastic martinis" made by the "old-school bartenders", "even if the tabs make you wish you were on an expense account."

	APPEAL	DECOR	SERVICE	COST

Bar None

| | 21 | 17 | 16 | $9 |

Yaletown | 1222 Hamilton St. (bet. Davie & Drake Sts.) | 604-689-7000 | www.dhmbars.ca

For "down-to-earth" dancing to "great live" R&B and soul, head to this "homey" club in a converted Yaletown warehouse that's recently added a VIP area; though acts can be "hit-or-miss", the "diverse, sexy" (if "slightly older") crowd is "fun" and "friendly."

Cascade Room, The

| | - | - | - | M |

East Side | 2616 Main St. (bet. 10th & 11th Aves.) | 604-709-8650 | www.thecascade.ca

Nick Devine (ex George) shakes things up in East Vancouver at this upbeat South Main sibling to restaurant/lounge Habit, with a 'local' style; a friendly crowd is packing in to sample the star mixologist's classic global tipples and to nibble from the menu of regional plates.

Ceili's Irish Pub & Restaurant

| | - | - | - | M |

Downtown | 670 Smithe St. (Granville St.) | 604-697-9199 | www.ceilis.com

More nightclub than pub, this Downtowner in the heart of the Entertainment District is one of the city's largest, with three Irish-themed floors, live music most nights and no shortage of special events; a lively mixed crowd packs in for casual food on one level, while others aim for the giant upstairs patio with fireplaces, heat lamps and a retractable roof that opens to the summer night sky.

Celebrities

| | 21 | 21 | 19 | $11 |

West End | 1022 Davie St. (bet. Burrard & Thurlow Sts.) | 604-681-6180 | www.celebritiesnightclub.com

"Where gay guys go to party and straight girls go to dance", this "fantastic" "mixed club" in the West End draws "all kinds of people"; regulars recommend the "upper viewing level" at this "Vancouver legend" where you can look down on a crowd grooving "on the wild side (or at least a little more open-mindedly)" to "music that kicks."

Cellar Nightclub

| | 18 | 18 | 19 | $10 |

Downtown | 1006 Granville St. (Nelson St.) | 604-605-4350 | www.cellarvan.com

With "great" rock bands and "bartenders that you want to take home", this "high-end" Downtown club below Doolin's Irish Pub attracts a "hot", "younger crowd"; you "do feel like you're in a cellar", albeit a "stylish, urban" one – just beware, the joint is also "a true meat market."

Z Commodore Ballroom, The
26 | 24 | 21 | $10

Downtown | 868 Granville St. (bet. Robson & Smithe Sts.) | 604-739-4550

"My dad used to swing here during World War II" say fans of this 1929 Downtown "institution", "the best live venue" for "any big event"; the "sprung floor" makes "jumping up and down" "so much fun", and with a "friendly staff", "it's no mystery why" it's "been popular for so long."

George Ultra Lounge
- | - | - | E

Yaletown | 1137 Hamilton St. (bet. Davie & Helmcken Sts.) | 604-628-5555 | www.georgelounge.com

A favourite with both Yaletown's after-work crowd and late-evening club-resisters, this London-inspired lounge draws fans for its edgy and classic cocktails; a well-stocked wine cellar paired with small and large plates courtesy of upstairs restaurant partner Brix staves off dinner cravings, while privacy-seekers head for the discreet G Spot nook.

Ginger Sixty Two
21 | 22 | 16 | $8

Downtown | 1219 Granville St. (bet. Davie & Drake Sts.) | 604-688-5494 | www.ginger62.com

The "hot crowd without all the little kiddies is a bonus" at this "sexy" '60s-inspired Downtowner with an "intimate feel"; start the evening with global small plates, and "don't expect to get in if you come too late" because this "casual-but-upscale" joint is a "favourite place to cool out."

900 West Lounge
20 | 23 | 18 | $12

Downtown | Fairmont Hotel Vancouver | 900 W. Georgia St. (bet. Burrard & Hornby Sts.) | 604-684-3131 | www.fairmont.com

Suits and suitors alike appreciate this "fine, functional" lounge Downtown in the historic Fairmont that's a "pretty" spot "for a drink or two" and "good bar snacks"; it's "appropriate for business meetings" when "you don't want too informal an atmosphere", but the setting is also "romantic" enough "to start or end the night with someone special."

	APPEAL	DECOR	SERVICE	COST

Odyssey

| | 17 | 12 | 14 | $8 |

Downtown | 1251 Howe St. (bet. Davie & Drake Sts.) | 604-689-5256 | www.theodysseynightclub.com

"Don't miss the <u>Shower Power show" on Thursdays</u> at this Downtown "techno" club/cabaret where "gorgeous" "older" guys come for drag queens, male strippers and partying; "the big fish in a small pond of gay nightlife options", it still has a few fussy fellows finding it "pretty scuzzy."

☑ Opus Bar

| | 23 | 23 | 20 | $14 |

Yaletown | Opus Hotel | 322 Davie St. (bet. Hamilton & Mainland Sts.) | 604-642-6787 | www.opushotel.com

"Keep your paparazzi eyes open" at this "movie star" "hangout" in Yaletown; an "upscale lounge with abundant eye candy", it's "so trendy you'll want to spit" – just don't get so caught up with celebs that you forget to "<u>monitor your date on the bathroom TVs</u>."

Railway Club, The

| | 24 | 18 | 17 | $8 |

Downtown | 579 Dunsmuir St. (Seymour St.) | 604-681-1625 | www.therailwayclub.com

Hop aboard for "all the best local bands" – from "up-and-coming acts" to "established alternative" groups – at this Downtown venue; it's a "favourite" "hip arts-scene hangout" for "all ages" who appreciate the "unpretentious atmosphere" and a staff that "makes you feel welcome."

Rossini's

| | - | - | - | E |

West Side | 1525 Yew St. (bet. Cornwall & York Aves.) | 604-737-8080 | www.rossinisjazz.com

"When there's a smokin' jazz combo playing", this West Side spot has a "great atmosphere" for dinner and live tunes; it may be more Italian "restaurant and lounge than nightclub", but it's quite "nice."

Shark Club

| | 20 | 17 | 16 | $7 |

Downtown | 180 W. Georgia St. (bet. Beatty & Cambie Sts.) | 604-687-4275
Langley | 20169 88 Ave. (202 St.) | 604-513-8600
www.sharkclubs.com

"Grab a brew" and "whoop it up" at these "laid-back" sports bars that succeed when they "stick to the basics" of "TV, cold draft and reliable meals"; later, they turn into "high-end" clubs, but for game sharks, they're mostly about "the Canucks getting their butts kicked."

	APPEAL	DECOR	SERVICE	COST

Yale Hotel, The

20 | 14 | 16 | $8

Downtown | 1300 Granville St. (Drake St.) | 604-681-9253 |
www.theyale.ca

The "rough-around-the-edges" room may "need a revamp", but it "fits
the music" at this "historic blues bar" in an 1885 building Downtown
that "brings in world-class acts"; it's "not too pretty", but it's cheap.

Victoria & Vancouver Island

Bengal Lounge

28 | 28 | 24 | $18

Downtown | Fairmont Empress Hotel | 721 Government St. (bet. Belleville &
Humboldt Sts.) | Victoria | 250-389-2727 | www.fairmont.com

"You'd think you were in colonial India" at this "ritzy" Downtowner, a
"historic place" to sip a signature Bengal Tiger cocktail "as you listen
to live jazz" on weekends and imagine you're "rich and famous"; it's
"not where you want to buy your own drink", but the "combination of
ale on draft with the day's curry" (from the buffet) is "pure heaven."

Shark Club

20 | 17 | 16 | $7

Downtown | 2852 Douglas St. (bet. Garbally Rd. & Market St.) | Victoria |
250-386-5888 | www.sharkclubs.com

See review in Vancouver Directory.

Sticky Wicket Pub & Restaurant

∇ 22 | 21 | 21 | $9

Downtown | Strathcona Hotel | 919 Douglas St. (Courtney St.) |
Victoria | 250-383-7137 | www.strathconahotel.com

"People of all ages" go to bat for this "huge", "friendly" pub, one of
seven sports-themed rooms in Victoria's "biggest conglomeration of
clubs", all in the Strathcona Hotel; it's "a great place" to "sit with
friends" and "watch all the strangeness go by" Downtown.

Whistler

Dubh Linn Gate Irish Pub

23 | 18 | 17 | $9

Whistler | Pan Pacific Mountainside | 4320 Sundial Cres.
(off Blackcomb Way) | 604-905-4047 | www.dubhlinngate.com

Just "steps from the gondola" in the Pan Pacific Lodge, this "hangout" is
"a perfect place to relish a pint of Guinness after a day on the slopes";
there's a "superb selection of beers", so "it's the right idea" "for a quick
drink or a long evening", even if the "faux"-Irish setting is "antiseptic."

	APPEAL	DECOR	SERVICE	COST

Garibaldi Lift Co. Bar & Grill (aka GLC)

| 23 | 19 | 18 | $10 |

Whistler | 4165 Springs Ln. (Whistler Way) | 604-905-2220

"Watch skiers finish their runs, cheer on your favourite sports team" or sit "beside the fireplace" and listen to live music at this slopeside bar above the gondola base that's "one of the best après-ski locales" in Whistler; it "attracts a mature crowd", perhaps because it's "not so much a nightclub as a place to lounge."

Longhorn Saloon

| 20 | 15 | 15 | $11 |

Whistler | Carleton Lodge | 4284 Mountain Sq. (Horstman Ln.) | 604-932-5999 | www.longhornsaloon.ca

The "huge patio" "fills up" at this Carleton Lodge "favourite for après ski"; "get there early" and "head to the bar to order your own drinks" because the "slow" staff "has a hard time getting around" the hordes.

Savage Beagle

| - | - | - | M |

Whistler | Blackcomb Lodge | 4222 Village Sq. (Sea to Sky Hwy.) | 604-938-3337 | www.savagebeagle.com

Inventive custom cocktails set the stage at this pumped upstairs-downstairs, long-running Whistler Village haunt that draws a fetching après crowd of lively regulars for its spirited list that also includes single malts and vintage cellar picks; celebrants may opt to party late in the lounge, or descend to the dance club, featuring some of the hippest DJs around.

SITES & ATTRACTIONS DIRECTORY

Sites & Attractions

Ratings & Symbols

Appeal, Facilities and **Service** are rated on the Zagat 0 to 30 scale.

Cost reflects the attraction's high-season price range (in Candadian dollars) for one adult admission, indicated as follows:

$0	Free		E	$26 to $40
I	$10 and below		VE	$41 or above
M	$11 to $25			

Vancouver

MOST POPULAR

1. Stanley Park
2. Vancouver Aquarium
3. Museum of Anthro./UBC
4. Capilano Bridge
5. Dr. Sun Yat-Sen/Gdn.

TOP APPEAL

27 Stanley Park
26 Museum of Anthro./UBC
   Vancouver Aquarium
25 Telus World of Science
24 VanDusen Botanical

Burnaby Village Museum
23 | 23 | 23 | M

Burnaby | 6501 Deer Lake Ave. (bet. Canada Way & Deer Lake Pl.) | 604-293-6500 | www.burnabyvillagemuseum.ca

Visitors to this "gorgeous" Burnaby living-history museum take a "walk back in time" in a 1920s village, complete with a restored carousel and a working blacksmith's forge; a "friendly staff and volunteers" add to the experience, though some quibble that this "small" site is "more of a pit stop than an ultimate destination for a kids' day out."

Capilano Suspension Bridge
23 | 20 | 17 | E

North Vancouver | 3735 Capilano Rd. | 604-985-7474 | www.capbridge.com

"Not for the faint of heart", a walk across this "swaying bridge" "nuzzling the towering pines" above the Capilano River "quickens the pulse"; thrill-seekers on "a natural high" feel like they're "on top of the world", but unimpressed amblers argue that it costs "too much money" when you can "head to Lynn Canyon's" span and get "the same feeling for free."

	APPEAL	FACIL.	SERVICE	COST

Dr. Sun Yat-Sen Classical Chinese Garden

22	20	17	I

Chinatown | 578 Carrall St. (bet. Keefer Pl. & W. Pender St.) | 604-662-3207 | www.vancouverchinesegarden.com

"An oasis of calm" on the edge of "bustling" Chinatown, this "classical Chinese garden", with its "little winding paths", "beautiful rock" arrangements and "fascinating botanicals", is a "contemplative" spot; "bring your camera", take a tour (the guides' "knowledge, history and perspective make the trip worthwhile") and "access your Zen-like state"; N.B. closed on Mondays November–April.

Granville Island

–	–	–	$0

Granville Island | Anderson St. (under the Granville St. Bridge) | 604-666-5784 | www.granvilleisland.com

Anchored by the foodie's paradise of the Public Market, this pedestrian-friendly peninsula that was once an industrial wasteland on the West Side is now a top attraction; browse the eclectic galleries, museums, theatres, restaurants and marine supply stores, or simply admire the city views from the shores of False Creek.

Grouse Mountain

–	–	–	VE

North Vancouver | 6400 Nancy Greene Way (Grousewoods Dr.) | 604-980-9311 | www.grousemountain.com

Its lights and Eye of the Wind energy tower visible for miles around, this North Vancouver peak with stunning panoramas and an array of activities is only a 15-minute drive from Downtown; you can ride the tram to ski day or night during December through April, take in a lumberjack show or go hiking, then rest up from all the action by hanging out on the picturesque patio at Altitude Bistro.

Museum of Anthropology at UBC

26	25	21	I

West Side | University of British Columbia | 6393 NW Marine Dr. (bet. E. Mall & W. Mall) | 604-822-5087 | www.moa.ubc.ca

Amateur ethnographers seeking "a crash course" in local "aboriginal history" "could spend days and only scratch the surface" of this "scholars' treasure trove" housed in Arthur Erickson's "stunning" West Side masterpiece on the University of British Columbia campus; "fabulous totem poles", "phenomenal" artifacts, the "spectacular" longhouse and world-famous sculptor Bill Reid's 'The Raven and the First Men' make it "a must-see"; completely open after a major renovation except for the temporary exhibit galley expected to be completed by January 2010.

⚡ Stanley Park

27 | 22 | 18 | $0

West End | Entrances at Beach Ave. (Lagoon Dr.) and W. Georgia St. (Chilco St.) | 604-681-6728 | www.www.vancouver.ca/parks/parks/stanley

"Bring your walking shoes" to this "jewel in Vancouver's crown", a "serene urban oasis" where the mountain views are "breathtaking" and the ways to enjoy yourself are "endless"; West End locals who "love it" for "hiking, biking, swimming and sunning" (and who voted it Vancouver's Most Popular attraction) suggest that whether you "walk the seawall" or "just hang out", it's "the essence of what this great city is all about."

Telus World of Science

25 | 24 | 22 | M

East Side | 1455 Quebec St. (Terminal Ave.) | 604-443-7443 | www.scienceworld.bc.ca

"Your kids go wild" amidst the "wonderful" "interactive displays" "that make learning cool" in this "spherical" East Side building that "looks like a giant golf ball at the end of False Creek"; it's a "great way to spend a rainy afternoon", especially if you take in an "amazing" IMAX show – just "try to go on a quiet day" because "it can be a zoo."

⚡ Vancouver Aquarium
Marine Science Centre

26 | 24 | 21 | M

West End | Stanley Park | 845 Avison Way (Aquarium Way) | 604-659-3521 | www.vanaqua.org

"Don't expect killer whales playing the tuba" – the "entertaining" yet "informative" exhibits are "designed for education" at Stanley Park's "compact", "captivating" marine facility; the "expert trainers" display "a lot of concern for the animals", and the place is "packed with things to do", so plan to spend at least "half a day interacting" with the "delightfully fun sea otters" and "humanlike belugas" at this "kids' favourite."

Vancouver Art Gallery

23 | 22 | 19 | M

Downtown | 750 Hornby St. (bet. Robson & W. Georgia Sts.) | 604-662-4719 | www.vanartgallery.bc.ca

From the "first-rate temporary exhibits" to a permanent collection that's strong on "fabulous" works by BC artist Emily Carr, "the curators do a wonderful job" at this "lovely" Downtown museum; though

APPEAL | FACIL. | SERVICE | COST

size queens "wish it were bigger", admirers assert that it's "attractive for locals and world travellers alike", particularly if you refuel in the "great cafe" or go on a pay-what-you-wish Tuesday evening.

Vancouver Maritime Museum
22 | 20 | 19 | M

West Side | 1905 Ogden Ave. (Chestnut St.) | 604-257-8300 | www.vancouvermaritimemuseum.com

A "must-see for kids" (or anyone) "with an interest in ships", this small but "surprisingly" good West Side waterfront museum is "a unique attraction with interesting, novel" marine exhibits; a highlight is a climb aboard the historic schooner St. Roch, the first vessel to navigate the Northwest Passage both ways; N.B. closed on Mondays.

Vancouver Museum
∇ 20 | 20 | 20 | M

West Side | Vanier Park | 1100 Chestnut St. (Whyte St.) | 604-736-4431 | www.museumofvancouver.ca

In the West Side's Vanier Park, this "interesting" museum with a cone-shaped roof that resembles a Coast Salish hat explores "everything on the origins of the West Coast"; a staff that's "passionate about Canadian history" channels enthusiasm into the "unique displays", so if critics crab that it's "not world-class", it's still "one of Vancouver's little-known gems"; N.B. closed on Mondays.

VanDusen Botanical Garden
24 | 21 | 20 | I

West Side | 5251 Oak St. (W. 37th Ave.) | 604-878-9274 | www.vandusengarden.org

"You can count on beauty each time you visit" the "peaceful", "well-kept grounds" of this "fantastic" West Side "treasure" filled with "rare, delicate" plants; "bring a picnic" or enjoy a "romantic" meal in the "quaint" Shaughnessy Restaurant, but don't miss the "awesome spring flower expositions", the "great" Elizabethan maze or December's "wonderful" Festival of Lights.

Victoria & Vancouver Island

☒ Butchart Gardens, The
28 | 26 | 22 | E

Brentwood Bay | 800 Benvenuto Ave. (Wallace Dr.) | 866-652-4422 | www.butchartgardens.com

This "virtual fairyland of flowers" is a "don't-miss", ranking among "the most magnificent" of its kind with "beautiful botanical displays" that include a "breathtaking Sunken Garden"; Saanich's patch of "pure heaven" is a "lovely place to walk", and since "children have endless [expanses] to explore", it's "not just for old codgers"; an "elaborate" afternoon tea is served in the Dining Room, and it's "worth a second trip" in summer for the Saturday night fireworks.

Butterfly Gardens

| 22 | 20 | 19 | M |

Brentwood Bay | 461 Benvenuto Ave. (Garden Gate Dr.) | 250-652-3822 | 877-722-0272 | www.butterflygardens.com

"Remember your camera" when you visit this "small but charming" tropical Saanich showcase where "exotic" butterflies "land on your hand"; "dress lightly" since "it can get hot and humid in the observatory", and "bring your kiddies" – unless flying insects "creep them out"; N.B. closed in January.

Craigdarroch Castle

| 23 | 22 | 21 | M |

Victoria | 1050 Joan Cres. (bet. Fort St. & Rockland Ave.) | 250-592-5323 | www.craigdarrochcastle.com

Luckily for her, the wife of Robert Dunsmuir (the BC coal baron who built this "imposing" mansion) "wasn't expected to vacuum", though she probably enjoyed the "gorgeous views from the top floor", and she might've liked the "excellent" self-guided tours nowadays; this "fascinating" 1890s building a 30-minute walk from Downtown is full of "good stories", but it's especially "beautiful" when decorated "during the holidays."

Royal British Columbia Museum

| 27 | 27 | 22 | M |

Victoria | 675 Belleville St. (bet. Douglas & Government Sts.) | 888-447-7977 | www.royalbcmuseum.bc.ca

Visitors "of all ages" "soak up all that is West Coast Canada" in the "spectacular exhibits" at this "wonderful" Downtown museum, a "winner" for "sensory delight"; the "outstanding First Nations items" and "dioramas alone are worth the price of admission", and the natural history section (with its "infamous wooly mammoth") is "excellent", so "take all day" to explore this "national treasure."

HOTEL
DIRECTORY

Hotels

Ratings & Symbols

Rooms, Service, Dining and **Facilities** are rated on the Zagat 0 to 30 scale.

Cost reflects the hotel's high-season rate (in Canadian dollars) for a standard double room. It does not reflect seasonal changes.

- 👫 children's programs
- ✗ exceptional restaurant
- Ⓗ historic interest
- ✂ kitchens
- 🐾 allows pets
- 👀 views

- ⚲ 18-hole golf course
- Ⓢ notable spa facilities
- ⛷ downhill skiing
- 🏊 swimming pool
- 🎾 tennis

Vancouver

Fairmont Hotel Vancouver, The ✗Ⓗ🐾👀Ⓢ🏊

| 21 | 24 | 21 | 22 | $219 |

Downtown | 900 W. Georgia St. | (1-604) 684-3131 | fax 662-1929 | 866-540-4452 | www.fairmont.com | 520 rooms, 36 suites

Emanating "old-world elegance" from the "grand lobby" to the "traditional" "English-style rooms", this 1939 "landmark" is "perfectly situated", particularly if you're on "a shopaholic's holiday"; the "cordial" staff "spoils you in the best ways", and "power diners" and drinkers convene at Griffins restaurant and 900 West Lounge, but "like an old lady trying to keep up", this "dowager" sure works hard for her "charms."

Fairmont Vancouver Airport 🐾👀Ⓢ🏊

| 27 | 25 | 22 | 24 | $219 |

Richmond | 3111 Grant McConachie Way | (1-604) 207-5200 | fax 248-3219 | 866-540-4441 | www.fairmont.com | 390 rooms, 2 suites

"If only all airport hotels were this nice" sigh sojourners smiling over this "utterly sybaritic" spot where the "vast", "whisper-quiet" rooms are "surprisingly contemporary" (baths are a "sea of beige marble") and you can "plane-watch from the floor-to-ceiling windows"; there's "nothing like a Jacuzzi and a visit to the excellent spa to while-away a stopover" say some who are so impressed by the "cool pool" and "wonderful service" that they'd "spend a week here."

Fairmont Waterfront, The ⊕ 🛁 🏨 🏊

ROOMS	SERVICE	DINING	FACIL.	COST
25	24	21	24	$219

Downtown | 900 Canada Place Way | (1-604) 691-1991 | fax 691-1999 | 866-540-4509 | www.fairmont.com | 459 rooms, 30 suites

Morgan, "the resident mutt", "welcomes" guests to this cruise-shipper favourite, "conveniently" located across from the "huge" Downtown port; "spectacular views" of the bay, mountains, city and Stanley Park distinguish the "well-appointed" (if "unimaginative") rooms, and help "set this apart from Fairmont's other" local offerings; the "near-perfect" service – "particularly" on the "Gold Level" – also draws raves.

Four Seasons ✕ 🛁 🏨 🏊

ROOMS	SERVICE	DINING	FACIL.	COST
23	26	23	23	$343

Downtown | 791 W. Georgia St. | (1-604) 689-9333 | fax 684-4555 | www.fourseasons.com | 306 rooms, 70 suites

"Not once will you hear a 'no'" from the "superb" staff that's "up to the chain's usual exemplary standards" at this "lovely" lodging in a "terrific location" with "easy access to Vancouver's Downtown core"; renovations to the rooms, lobby and the "fantastic" Yew restaurant were recently completed.

NEW Loden Vancouver Hotel 🛁 🏨

ROOMS	SERVICE	DINING	FACIL.	COST
–	–	–	–	$399

Downtown | 1177 Melville St. | (1-604) 563-3622 | fax 373-1609 | www.lodenvancouver.com | 70 rooms

This discreet, luxurious, contemporary-style boutique property tucked away on a quiet side street close to the Downtown core is known for its personalised touches such as in-room spa services and on-call personal trainers, as well as complimentary cars available for guests; dining is highlighted by the modern, Regency-styled Voya restaurant with a private room for up to 18 and cutting-edge cocktails in the 50-seat lounge.

Opus Hotel ✕ 🛁

ROOMS	SERVICE	DINING	FACIL.	COST
24	26	21	21	$239

Yaletown | 322 Davie St. | (1-604) 642-6787 | fax 642-6780 | 866-642-6787 | www.opushotel.com | 84 rooms, 12 suites

"Put the blinds down in the W/C" since there are some "street-facing bathrooms" at this "one-of-a-kind" boutique hotel in "trendy" Yaletown – "the place in Vancouver to see and be seen"; from the "refreshingly" "hip" accommodations, done in a rainbow of "funky", vibrant hues, to the "hot" lobby bar where you're apt to "run into movie stars" to the classic French brasserie, Elixir's, the scene is "sexy and modern."

Pacific Palisades

▽ 20	21	15	20	$200

Downtown | 1277 Robson St. | (1-604) 688-0461 | fax 688-4374 | 800-663-1815 | www.pacificpalisadeshotel.com | 232 suites

Fans of the Miami "retro look" go gaga for the "quirky decor" and "bold colors" at this "fun" spot, where the "spacious suites" – like "furnished apartments" – are "comfortable, especially for longer stays" and you'll have "terrific views of the Vancouver skyline" if your room is high enough; run by a "helpful staff", it's a "true value" just off "the best shopping street in town."

Pan Pacific

25	24	23	25	$540

Downtown | 300-999 Canada Pl. | (1-604) 662-8111 | fax 685-8690 | 877-324-4856 | www.panpacific.com | 465 rooms, 39 suites

With an "incredible location" on "Vancouver's waterfront", this favourite of "conventions" and "the cruise-ship crowd" is best loved for its "spectacular views" of the harbour and Stanley Park; inside, "modern" rooms, a stellar spa and gym and "first-rate service" make this one of the most "consistently high-quality" spots in town; P.S. they can be "generous with upgrades" for those "not part of a big group."

🆕 Shangri-La Hotel Vancouver

–	–	–	–	$345

Downtown | 1128 W. Georgia St. | (1-604) 689-1120 | fax 689-1195 | www.shangri-la.com | 80 rooms, 39 suites

Downtown's newest anchor and the city's tallest tower is home to Shangri-La's first foray into North America, with 119 luxurious suites and rooms in the heart of the city, many with balconies and panoramic views, surrounded by every convenience; Asian-accented guestrooms feature floor-to-ceiling windows, remote-controlled blinds and natural-light bathrooms with triple-head walk in-showers; other amenities range from the CHI Spa to regional fine French dining in the upscale Market by Jean-Georges, and flexible meeting and reception spaces for groups of up to 110.

	ROOMS	SERVICE	DINING	FACIL.	COST

Sutton Place Hotel ❄️🍴Ⓢ🏊

| 24 | 25 | 23 | 22 | $288 |

Downtown | 845 Burrard St. | (1-604) 682-5511 | fax 682-5513 | 866-378-8866 | www.suttonplace.com | 350 rooms, 47 suites

"Canadian hospitality at its finest" distinguishes this "lively, up-scale" Downtown destination, which draws surveyor raves for its "fabulous", "attitude-less" staff and concierge and – thanks to its popularity with "Hollywood North" – "star-sightings galore"; near the "active lobby", the Fleuri restaurant serves "fine food" and "a chocolate-lover's buffet to die for", while upstairs, "immaculate" rooms have a "European feel."

Wedgewood Ⓢ

| 24 | 26 | 24 | 22 | $500 |

Downtown | 845 Hornby St. | (1-604) 689-7777 | fax 608-5348 | 800-663-0666 | www.wedgewoodhotel.com | 41 rooms, 42 suites

"A little bit of Europe" "in the heart of Vancouver", this "charming" boutique "favourite" makes you feel like you're "staying with a wealthy socialite aunt" who knows just how to make the "mixed crowd" "feel comfortable"; many of the "understated" rooms feature jetted tubs, while the fully renovated Penthouse suites are "lovely"; add in the "exceptional staff", "decent spa", "fabulous bar and restaurant" and "yummy cookies" "at turndown", and there's "no need to leave."

Westin Bayshore ❄️🍴🏊

| 23 | 23 | 19 | 22 | $514 |

Downtown | 1601 Bayshore Dr. | (1-604) 682-3377 | fax 687-3102 | 888-219-2157 | www.westin.com | 511 rooms

"Jog out the back door" to the seawall for an "exceptional" workout, when you stay at this sprawling property on Coal Harbour, just "a stone's throw from Stanley Park"; it has "beautiful views of the marina and the mountains", "well-appointed rooms" and business-friendly service, as well as "great conference facilities."

Westin Grand 🐕❄️🍴Ⓢ🏊

| 24 | 20 | 17 | 21 | $449 |

Downtown | 433 Robson St. | (1-604) 602-1999 | fax 647-2502 | 800-937-8461 | www.westingrandvancouver.com | 207 suites

You might not realize that this "chic" "all-suite hotel" is "shaped like a grand piano", but you will notice it's got a "clever design", including "practical" mini-kitchens tucked into the walls; athletic types "love the fitness facilities and outdoor pool", sybarites appreciate the spa and the city center location is "excellent for business."

ROOMS | SERVICE | DINING | FACIL. | COST

Victoria & Vancouver Island

Aerie Resort ✕🛏🐾⑤🔍
25 | 26 | 24 | 24 | $259

Malahat | 600 Ebedora Ln. | (1-250) 743-7115 | fax 743-4766 |
800-518-1933 | www.aerie.bc.ca | 9 rooms, 26 suites
"Divine location, views and dining" sum up this "beautiful" Relais &
Châteaux "haven on Vancouver Island", an "out-of-the-way" retreat
just 30 minutes from Victoria that seems like a world away; propo-
nents praise the "impeccable service" and "lovely rooms with balconies overlooking the forest", advising "get a suite with a sunken tub."

Fairmont
Empress, The 🚶⑪🛏🐾⚓⑤⛱
21 | 25 | 23 | 24 | $299

Victoria | 721 Government St. | (1-250) 384-4334 | fax 381-4334 |
866-540-4429 | www.fairmont.com | 441 rooms, 36 suites
You'll "step back in time" as you enter this "incredibly beautiful"
British "landmark" with "gorgeous" Inner Harbour views, a
"postcard-perfect" setting and a "can-do" staff; it takes "plenty of
walking" to "get anywhere" inside this "rambling" hotel, but find your
way to the "best high tea" ("you must try it before you're dead") and
the "lovely blue tile pool"; even if some complain this "grand lady" is
"stuffy", she's still the "queen of hotels in British Columbia" and "not
just a tourist destination."

Grand Pacific, Hotel 🛏🐾⑤⛱
▽ 24 | 25 | 21 | 22 | $279

Victoria | 463 Belleville St. | (1-250) 386-0450 | fax 380-4475 |
800-663-7550 | www.hotelgrandpacific.com | 258 rooms, 46 suites
"A saving grace in Victoria", this imposing, pink-tinged lodging
with châteaulike gables is blessed with an "excellent location on
the Inner Harbour" as well as "service that's eager to please"; all
rooms and suites have balconies, and other amenities include extensive banquet and meeting rooms, a spa and a health club with
a pool, though some say the on-site dining "isn't quite up to the
hotel's overall standards."

Hastings House ✕🐾⑤
24 | 27 | 29 | 20 | $495

Salt Spring Island | 160 Upper Ganges Rd. | (1-250) 537-2362 |
fax 537-5333 | 800-661-9255 | www.hastingshouse.com | 18 suites
Hedonists experience "sinful comfort" at this "tranquil" lodging
situated in "one of the most magical places on the planet", a few hours

away from Vancouver on Salt Spring Island; accommodations are situated in hillside suites or a cosy 1938 manor house and there are "spectacular" water views, lush grounds and a sculpture garden, but it's the "outstanding food" that "alone is worth the trip"; P.S. "bring a titanium credit card."

Sooke Harbour House ✥▥ | 25 | 26 | 27 | 21 | $419 |

Sooke | 1528 Whiffen Spit Rd. | (1-250) 642-3421 | fax 642-6988 | www.sookeharbourhouse.com | 11 rooms, 17 suites

Surrounded by the Pacific Ocean and colourful gardens, this "serene and sophisticated" inn on Vancouver Island, 45 minutes away from Victoria, gets the nod for "unobstructed views of the harbour" and "outstanding gourmet cuisine"; "cosy" quarters are "individual works of art" with antiques, rock fireplaces, a bottle of port and several pairs of rainboots to encourage exploration of the extensive grounds.

Westin Bear Mountain Victoria Golf Resort & Spa, The ✕⌂✥▥⌐◷≋ | – | – | – | – | $389 |

Victoria | 1999 Country Club Way | (1-250) 391-7160 | fax 391-3792 | 888-533-2327 | www.bearmountain.ca | 86 rooms, 70 suites

Duffers are the target audience of this resort set on the fairways of the Bear Mountain Golf and Country Club, co-designed by Jack and Steve Nicklaus; rooms have views of the course and of Mount Finlayson, and feature deep-soaking tubs, natural slate flooring and balconies or terraces; other amenities include a pool, a spa and a fitness center; N.B. a second course has opened.

Wickaninnish Inn ✕✥▥◷ | 27 | 26 | 26 | 26 | $500 |

Tofino | 500 Osprey Ln. | (1-250) 725-3100 | fax 725-3110 | 800-333-4604 | www.wickinn.com | 63 rooms, 12 suites

"When you really want to get away" come to this "spectacular" Relais & Châteaux "dream of a place" on the rugged coast of Vancouver Island with "delightful" rooms where you can "lay in bed looking out" at the "fabulous views over the Pacific" or enjoying your private fireplace; the "first-class" staff's "attention to detail is astounding", and the "excellent" food extends to an all-you-can-eat "crab cookout on the beach that's not to be missed" – it's "wild", "wonderful" and definitely "worth the trek."

	ROOMS	SERVICE	DINING	FACIL.	COST

Whistler

Adara Hotel 🏨♨☆

| - | - | - | - | $299 |

Whistler | 4122 Village Green | (1-604) 905-4009 | 866-502-3272 |
www.adarahotel.com | 21 rooms, 20 suites

A playful design with plenty of natural accents is the highlight of this
stylish boutique right near the Whistler and Blackcomb Mountain gon-
dolas; rooms come with spa-like baths and 'floating' fireplaces, and facilities include an outdoor heated pool (seasonal), a year-round hot
tub with mountain views and a large lobby with fireplace.

Fairmont Chateau Whistler, The 🏌🏨♨⬆☺☆☆🔍

| 24 | 25 | 22 | 26 | $350 |

Whistler | 4599 Chateau Blvd. | (1-604) 938-8000 | fax 938-2291 |
800-606-8244 | www.fairmont.com | 493 rooms, 57 suites

The "only work you have to do" at this "fantastic" ski-in/ski-out resort
"at the foot" of Blackcomb Mountain is shoosh down the slopes – "everything else is done for you" by an "affable", "impeccable" staff that
goes "above and beyond" (it'll even "chase away the bears"); it's a
"beautiful summer destination" too, since the "top-notch facilities" include a Robert Trent Jones Jr.–designed golf course, dining that "beats
anything in town" and the "best bar."

Four Seasons 🏌🏨♨☺☆

| 28 | 28 | 25 | 28 | $405 |

Whistler | 4591 Blackcomb Way | (1-604) 935-3400 | fax 935-3455 |
888-935-2460 | www.fourseasons.com | 183 rooms, 90 suites, 37 condos

As "champion of the region", this "incredibly posh" outpost of the venerable brand may be a "little farther than other resorts from the lifts" but
is still "perfect for après ski" with its "cosy lobby" and "gorgeous" pool
and hot tubs; reviewers swoon over the "ultramodern" rooms with in-
room fireplaces, the "excellent", though "exceedingly pricey", spa and
the "innovative" restaurant, but it's probably the signature service from
a "world-class" staff that makes this a truly "memorable experience."

Pan Pacific Whistler Village Centre 🏨♨☺☆☆

| 26 | 22 | 19 | 24 | $519 |

Whistler | 4229 Blackcomb Way | (1-604) 905-2999 | fax 966-5501 |
www.panpacific.com | 83 suites

In a "perfect location" in the middle of posh Whistler Village, this "fabulous" boutique offers a "stylish" setting with "amazing" facilities that

include "large" rooms with full kitchens, gas fireplaces and soaking tubs; a "stone's throw from all the action" with "everything you need for the ski trip of your dreams" (including "top-notch" service, a spa, outdoor hot tubs and a "stick-to-the-ribs breakfast"), this one is "worth every penny."

Westin
Resort & Spa 🏃🛏️🍴🏋️⬆️🕐🐾〰️

| | 24 | 22 | 20 | 26 | $529 |

Whistler | 4090 Whistler Way | (1-604) 905-5000 | fax 905-5640 | 888-634-5577 | www.westinwhistler.com | 419 suites

An all-suites example of "mountain-resort chic", this chain link "at the foot of the mountains", "next to lifts" and nightlife boasts "beautifully appointed" quarters that are more like "fully equipped apartments" with the "best beds on the slopes", kitchenettes and "push-button fireplaces"; other highlights at this "family-friendly" retreat include a spa and health club with a pool, "shuttle service around Whistler Village" and a "staff willing to accommodate" requests.

40,000 places to eat, drink, stay & play – free at ZAGAT.com

INDEXES

Dining Cuisines

Includes restaurant names, neighbourhoods and Food ratings. Dining locations outside Vancouver are marked as follows: V&V=Victoria & Vancouver Island; W=Whistler.

AMERICAN (NEW)

Crave | **E Side**   21

ASIAN

Flying Tiger | **W Side**   24

ASIAN FUSION

Stella's | **E Side**   20

BARBECUE

Memphis Blues BBQ | **multi.**   21

Smoken Bones | 23
  Langford/V&V

BELGIAN

Chambar | **Downtown**   26

BURGERS

Splitz Grill | **multi.**   19

Vera's Burger | **multi.**   20

CHINESE

(* dim sum specialist)
Imperial Chinese* | **Downtown**   23

J & J Wonton | 24
  Downtown/V&V

Kirin Mandarin* | **Downtown**   25

Kirin Seafood* | **multi.**   24

Sha-Lin Noodle House | **W Side**   20

Shanghai Chinese* | **Downtown**   22

Sun Sui Wah* | **multi.**   25

Szechuan Chongqing | **E Side**   20

Wild Rice | **Downtown**   23

CONTINENTAL

Z Edgewater Lodge | 23
  Whistler/W

NEW La Brasserie | **W End**   23

Pear Tree | **Burnaby**   25

CREOLE

Smoken Bones | 23
  Langford/V&V

DESSERT

Fleuri | **Downtown**   23

Griffins | **Downtown**   22

Trafalgar's Bistro | **W Side**   24

DINERS

Tomahawk BBQ | **N Vancouver**   21

ECLECTIC

Bin 941/942 | **multi.**   25

Blue Fox Cafe | **Downtown/V&V**   22

Cafe Medina | **Downtown**   24

NEW Edge Social Grille | **Downtown**	—
Elements | **Whistler/W**	25
glowbal grill | **Yaletown**	21
Habit Lounge | **E Side**	—
NEW Latitude on Main | **E Side**	—
Monk's Grill | **Whistler/W**	18
Nu | **Downtown**	21
NEW Pourhouse | **Gastown**	18
Rebar | **Downtown/V&V**	25
NEW Refinery | **Downtown**	20
NEW Revel Room | **Gastown**	20
NEW r.tl | **Yaletown**	25
Z Sobo | **Tofino/V&V**	27
Steamworks | **Gastown**	—
NEW Stella's/Cambie | **W Side**	16
Stella's | **E Side**	20
Trafalgar's Bistro | **W Side**	24
NEW Voya | **Downtown**	22

EUROPEAN (MODERN)

FigMint | **W Side**	19

FRENCH

Aerie Resort | **Malahat/V&V**	25
Amusé Bistro | **Shawnigan Lake/V&V**	23
Z NEW Au Petit Chavignol | **E Side**	26

Bacchus | **Downtown**	25
Boneta | **Gastown**	24
Cassis Bistro | **Downtown**	20
Deep Cove | **Sidney/V&V**	26
Z Five Sails | **Downtown**	24
Fleuri | **Downtown** dessert only	23
Hermitage | **Downtown**	25
Z La Belle Auberge | **Ladner**	28
NEW La Brasserie | **W End**	23
Z Le Crocodile | **Downtown**	27
Le Gavroche | **W End**	22
NEW Les Faux Bourgeois | **E Side**	23
Lumière | **W Side**	26
NEW Market/Jean-Georges | **Downtown**	26
Paprika Bistro | **Oak Bay/V&V**	27
Provence Marina | **Yaletown**	23
Provence | **W Side**	25
Rest. Matisse | **Downtown/V&V**	26

FRENCH (BISTRO)

Bacchus Bistro | **Langley**	24
Bistro Pastis | **W Side**	24
Bistrot Bistro | **W Side**	22
Z Brasserie L'Ecole | **Downtown/V&V**	27
Café de Paris | **W End**	21

NEW db Bistro Moderne | **W Side**	23
Elixir Bistro | **Yaletown**	23
Jules Bistro | **Gastown**	21
La Régalade | **W Vancouver**	26
Mistral Bistro | **W Side** *lunch prefix*	24
Pied-à-Terre | **W Side**	24
Salade de Fruits | **W Side** *cash only*	23

GERMAN

NEW La Brasserie | **W End**	23

GREEK

Kalamata Greek | **W Side**	21
Stepho's Souvlaki | **W End**	20
Takis Taverna | **W End**	23

INDIAN

Maurya Indian | **W Side**	21
Saravanaa | **W Side**	23
Z Vij's | **W Side**	28
Vij's Rangoli | **W Side**	26

IRISH

Irish Heather | **Gastown**	18

ITALIAN
(N=Northern; S=Southern)

Amarcord | **Yaletown**	22
Cafe Il Nido | **Downtown**	20
NEW Campagnolo | N | **E Side**	-
NEW Cibo Trattoria | **Downtown**	24
CinCin | **Downtown**	24
Don Francesco | **Downtown**	24
Il Caminetto | N | **Whistler/W**	24
Il Giardino | N | **Downtown**	26
Il Terrazzo | N | **Downtown/V&V**	24
Italian Kitchen | **Downtown**	20
La Buca | **W Side** *reservations*	26
NEW L'Altro Buca | **W End**	26
NEW La Quercia | **W Side**	25
La Terrazza | **Yaletown**	25
Lombardo's | **E Side**	20
Marcello | **E Side**	22
NEW Nook | **W End**	-
Pagliacci's | **Downtown/V&V**	21
Paprika Bistro | **Oak Bay/V&V**	27
NEW Pizzeria Prima | S | **Downtown/V&V**	21
Q4 | **W Side**	25
Quattro/Whistler | **Whistler/W**	23
Tratt. di Umberto | **Whistler/W**	24
NEW Tratt. Italian Kitchen | **W Side**	22
Water St. Café | **Gastown**	19
Zambri's | **Downtown/V&V**	26

JAPANESE

(* sushi specialist)

EN Japanese	W Side	24
Gyoza King	W End	24
Hapa Izakaya	multi.	22
Kingyo	W End	26
Kitanoya Guu	Downtown	26
Kobe	Downtown	22
NEW Miku*	Downtown	-
NEW Ping's Cafe	E Side	19
Shiro Japanese*	W Side	27
Sushi Village*	Whistler/W	23
Z ToJo's*	W Side	27
Toshi*	E Side	24

LEBANESE

Nuba	multi.	24

MALAYSIAN

Tropika Malaysian	multi.	20

MEDITERRANEAN

Caramba!	Whistler/W	18
Z Cioppino's	Yaletown	28
NEW Mis Trucos	W End	-
Moustache Café	N Vancouver	23
Provence	W Side	25
Stage	Downtown/V&V	26

MEXICAN

Lolita's Cantina	W End	22
Me & Julio	E Side	17
Topanga Cafe	W Side	21

NUEVO LATINO

Century	Downtown	19
Cobre	Gastown	22

PACIFIC NORTHWEST

Aerie Resort	Malahat/V&V	25
Aqua Riva	Downtown	20
Z Araxi	Whistler/W	26
Aubergine Grille	Whistler/W	24
NEW Aura	Downtown/V&V	24
Beach House	W Vancouver	22
Z Bear Foot Bistro	Whistler/W	27
Z Bishop's	W Side	27
Brix	Yaletown	21
Cafe Brio	Downtown/V&V	26
Camille's	Downtown/V&V	27
NEW Circa	Downtown	18
NEW Crave Beachside	W Vancouver	22
Cru	W Side prix fixe	25
Delilah's	W End	20
Diva at Met	Downtown	26
NEW Edge	Sooke/V&V	-
Z Edgewater Lodge	Whistler/W	23
Z Empress Rm.	Downtown/V&V	23
Fifty Two 80	Whistler/W	22
Z Five Sails	Downtown	24

DINING

CUISINES

Fraîche | **W Vancouver**	
Fuel | **W Side**	26
Globe @ YVR | **Richmond**	22
Goldfish | **Yaletown**	20
Griffins | **Downtown**	22
Habit Lounge | **E Side**	-
Haro's | **Sidney/V&V**	20
Hart House | **Burnaby**	21
☑ Hastings Hse. | **Salt Spring Is/V&V**	27
Herons | **Downtown**	23
Horizons/Burnaby | **Burnaby**	20
☑ La Rua | **Whistler/W**	25
Lift | **W End**	18
Marina | **Oak Bay/V&V**	21
Mountain Club | **Whistler/W**	21
Ocean Club | **W Vancouver**	22
O'Doul's | **Downtown**	22
☑ Panache | **Langford/V&V**	28
Pescatore | **Downtown/V&V**	20
Pointe/Wickaninnish | **Tofino/V&V**	25
Raincity Grill | **W End**	24
☑ Rim Rock | **Whistler/W**	26
Salmon House | **W Vancouver**	21
☑ Seasons In Park | **W Side**	23
So.cial | **Gastown**	18
☑ Sooke Harbour | **Sooke/V&V**	27

Tapastree | **W End**	24
Teahouse/Stanley Park | **W End**	23
Temple | **Downtown/V&V**	21
Tomato Fresh Food | **W Side**	17
NEW 2 Chefs/Table | **E Side**	19
Watermark/Kits | **W Side**	16
Water St. Café | **Gastown**	19
☑ West | **W Side**	27
Wildflower | **Whistler/W**	22
Wild Garlic | **W End**	24
Yew | **Downtown**	22

PACIFIC RIM

NEW Aura | **Downtown/V&V**	24

PIZZA

Lombardo's | **E Side**	20
Marcello | **E Side**	22
Nat's NY Pizzeria | **multi.**	22
NEW Pizzeria Prima | **Downtown/V&V**	21

PORTUGUESE

Senova | **W Side**	23

PUB FOOD

NEW Bard/Banker Public Hse. | **Downtown/V&V**	18
Cardero's | **W End**	18

SEAFOOD

Blue Crab	Downtown/V&V	23
☑ Blue Water Cafe	Yaletown	26
Cannery	E Side	23
Coast	W End	23
C Restaurant	Downtown	25
Ferris' Oyster Bar	Downtown/V&V	22
Fish House	W End	22
Go Fish!	W Side	25
Goldfish	Yaletown	20
Imperial Chinese	Downtown	23
Joe Fortes	Downtown	22
Kirin Seafood	multi.	24
Lure	Downtown/V&V	24
Marina	Oak Bay/V&V	21
Pajo's	multi.	21
Pescatore	Downtown/V&V	20
Red Fish	Downtown/V&V	25
☑ Rim Rock	Whistler/W	26
Rodney's Oyster	Yaletown	24
Shore Club	Downtown	20
Sun Sui Wah	multi.	25

SMALL PLATES
(See also Spanish tapas specialist)

☑ NEW Au Petit Chavignol	French	E Side	26
Bin 941/942	Eclectic	W End	25
Cru	Pac. NW	W Side	25
Elements	Eclectic	Whistler/W	25
NEW Mis Trucos	Med.	W End	–
NEW Ping's Cafe	Japanese	E Side	19
NEW Refinery	Eclectic	Downtown	20
NEW Revel Room	Eclectic	Gastown	20
NEW r.tl	Eclectic	Yaletown	25
Stage	Med.	Downtown/V&V	26
Stella's	Asian/Eclectic	E Side	20
Tapastree	Pac. NW	W End	24
NEW Voya	Eclectic	Downtown	22
Wild Garlic	Pac. NW	W End	24

SPANISH
(* tapas specialist)

Senova*	W Side	23

STEAKHOUSES

Gotham Steak	Downtown	24
Hy's Encore	Downtown	24
Hy's Steak	Whistler/W	23
Joe Fortes	Downtown	22
☑ Keg Steak	multi.	20
Kobe	Downtown	22
Saltlik Steak	Downtown	19
Shore Club	Downtown	20

DINING

CUISINES

SWISS

William Tell | **Downtown** *lunch* 22

THAI

NEW Maenam | **W Side** 26

Montri's Thai | **W Side** 23

Salathai Thai | **multi.** 20

Sawasdee Thai | **E Side** 22

Siam Thai | **Downtown/V&V** 21

Simply Thai | **Yaletown** 23

Tropika Malaysian | **multi.** 20

VEGETARIAN

Rebar | **Downtown/V&V** 25

Dining Locations

Includes restaurant names, cuisines and Food ratings.

Vancouver

BURNABY

Hart House	*Pac. NW*	21
Horizons/Burnaby	*Pac. NW*	20
☑ Keg Steak	*Steak*	20
Pear Tree	*Continental*	25

COQUITLAM

Kirin Seafood	*Chinese*	24

DOWNTOWN

Aqua Riva	*Pac. NW*	20
Bacchus	*French*	25
Cafe Il Nido	*Italian*	20
Cafe Medina	*Eclectic*	24
Cassis Bistro	*French*	20
Century	*Nuevo Latino*	19
Chambar	*Belgian*	26
NEW Cibo Trattoria	*Italian*	24
CinCin	*Italian*	24
NEW Circa	*Pac. NW*	18
C Restaurant	*Seafood*	25
Diva at Met	*Pac. NW*	26
Don Francesco	*Italian*	24
NEW Edge Social Grille	*Eclectic*	—
☑ Five Sails	*French/Pac. NW*	24

Fleuri	*French* *dessert only*	23
Gotham Steak	*Steak*	24
Griffins	*Pac. NW*	22
Hermitage	*French*	25
Herons	*Pac. NW*	23
Hy's Encore	*Steak*	24
Il Giardino	*Italian*	26
Imperial Chinese	*Chinese*	23
Italian Kitchen	*Italian*	20
Joe Fortes	*Seafood/Steak*	22
☑ Keg Steak	*Steak*	20
Kirin Mandarin	*Chinese*	25
Kitanoya Guu	*Japanese*	26
Kobe	*Japanese/Steak*	22
☑ Le Crocodile	*French*	27
NEW Market/Jean-Georges	*French* *lunch menu ONLY*	26
NEW Miku	*Japanese*	—
Nu	*Eclectic*	21
Nuba	*Lebanese*	24
O'Doul's	*Pac. NW*	22
NEW Refinery	*Eclectic*	20
Salathai Thai	*Thai*	20
Saltlik Steak	*Steak*	19
Shanghai Chinese	*Chinese*	22
Shore Club	*Seafood/Steak*	20

DINING

LOCATIONS

Tropika Malaysian	*SE Asian*	20		

GASTOWN

Tropika Malaysian	*SE Asian*	20
NEW Voya	*Eclectic*	22
Wild Rice	*Chinese*	23
William Tell	*Swiss* lunch	22
Yew	*Pac. NW*	22

EAST SIDE

Z NEW Au Petit Chavignol	*French*	26
NEW Campagnolo	*Italian*	-
Cannery	*Seafood*	23
Crave	*Amer.*	21
Habit Lounge	*Eclectic*	-
NEW Latitude on Main	*Eclectic*	-
NEW Les Faux Bourgeois	*French*	23
Lombardo's	*Italian/Pizza*	20
Marcello	*Italian/Pizza*	22
Me & Julio	*Mex.*	17
Memphis Blues BBQ	*BBQ*	21
NEW Ping's Cafe	*Japanese*	19
Sawasdee Thai	*Thai*	22
Splitz Grill	*Burgers*	19
Stella's	*Asian/Eclectic*	20
Sun Sui Wah	*Chinese/Seafood*	25
Szechuan Chongqing	*Chinese*	20
Toshi	*Japanese*	24
NEW 2 Chefs/Table	*Pac. NW*	19
Vera's Burger	*Burgers*	20

GASTOWN

Boneta	*French*	24
Cobre	*Nuevo Latino*	22
Irish Heather	*Irish*	18
Jules Bistro	*French*	21
Nuba	*Lebanese*	24
NEW Pourhouse	*Eclectic*	18
NEW Revel Room	*Eclectic*	20
Salt Tasting Room	*Deli*	23
So.cial	*Pac. NW*	18
Steamworks	*Eclectic*	-
Vera's Burger	*Burgers*	20
Water St. Café	*Italian/Pac. NW*	19

GRANVILLE ISLAND

Z Keg Steak	*Steak*	20

KELOWNA

Memphis Blues BBQ	*BBQ*	21

LADNER

Z La Belle Auberge	*French*	28

LANGLEY

Bacchus Bistro	*French*	24

NEW WESTMINSTER

Z Keg Steak	*Steak*	20
Kirin Seafood	*Chinese*	24

NORTH VANCOUVER

Memphis Blues BBQ	*BBQ*	21
Moustache Café	*Med.*	23

Tomahawk BBQ	*Diner*	21	NEW L'Altro Buca	*Italian*	26
Vera's Burger	*Burgers*	20	Le Gavroche	*French*	22
		Lift	*Pac. NW*	18

PORT MOODY

Pajo's | *Seafood* — 21

Lolita's Cantina | *Mex.* — 22

NEW Mis Trucos | *Med.* — -

RICHMOND

Globe @ YVR	*Pac. NW*	22	Nat's NY Pizzeria	*Pizza*	22
Z Keg Steak	*Steak*	20	NEW Nook	*Italian*	-
Kirin Seafood	*Chinese*	24	Raincity Grill	*Pac. NW*	24
Sun Sui Wah	*Chinese/Seafood*	25	Stepho's Souvlaki	*Greek*	20
Tropika Malaysian	*SE Asian*	20	Takis Taverna	*Greek*	23
		Tapastree	*Pac. NW*	24

DINING

STEVESTON

Pajo's | *Seafood* — 21

Teahouse/Stanley Park | *Pac. NW* — 23

Vera's Burger | *Burgers* — 20

SURREY

Z Keg Steak	*Steak*	20	Wild Garlic	*Pac. NW*	24
Memphis Blues BBQ	*BBQ*	21	

WEST END

WEST SIDE South Vancouver

Bin 941/942	*Eclectic*	25	Bin 941/942	*Eclectic*	25
Café de Paris	*French*	21	Z Bishop's	*Pac. NW*	27
Cardero's	*Pub*	18	Bistro Pastis	*French*	24
Coast	*Seafood*	23	Bistrot Bistro	*French*	22
Delilah's	*Pac. NW*	20	Cru	*Pac. NW* prix fixe	25
Fish House	*Seafood*	22	NEW db Bistro Moderne	*French*	23
Gyoza King	*Japanese*	24	EN Japanese	*Japanese*	24
Hapa Izakaya	*Japanese*	22	FigMint	*Euro.*	19
Kingyo	*Japanese*	26	Flying Tiger	*Asian*	24
NEW La Brasserie	*French/German*	23	Fuel	*Pac. NW*	26
		Go Fish!	*Seafood* ?	25

LOCATIONS

Hapa Izakaya | *Japanese* 22

Kalamata Greek | *Greek* 21

Kirin Seafood | *Chinese* 24

La Buca | *Italian* reservations 26

NEW La Quercia | *Italian* 25

Lumière | *French* 26

NEW Maenam | *Thai* 26

Maurya Indian | *Indian* 21

Memphis Blues BBQ | *BBQ* 21

Mistral Bistro | *French* lunch prefix 24

Montri's Thai | *Thai* 23

Nat's NY Pizzeria | *Pizza* 22

Pied-à-Terre | *French* 24

Provence | *French/Med.* 25

Q4 | *Italian* 25

Salade de Fruits | *French* cash only 23

Salathai Thai | *Thai* 20

Saravanaa | *Indian* 23

Z Seasons In Park | *Pac. NW* 23

Senova | *Portug./Spanish* 23

Sha-Lin Noodle House | *Chinese* 20

Shiro Japanese | *Japanese* 27

NEW Stella's/Cambie | *Eclectic* 16

Z ToJo's | *Japanese* 27

Tomato Fresh Food | *Pac. NW* 17

Topanga Cafe | *Mex.* 21

Trafalgar's Bistro | *Eclectic* 24

NEW Tratt. Italian Kitchen | *Italian* 22

Tropika Malaysian | *SE Asian* 20

Vera's Burger | *Burgers* 20

Z Vij's | *Indian* 28

Vij's Rangoli | *Indian* 26

Watermark/Kits | *Pac. NW* 16

Z West | *Pac. NW* 27

WEST VANCOUVER

Beach House | *Pac. NW* 22

NEW Crave Beachside | *Pacific NW* 22

Fraîche | *Pac. NW* 24

Z Keg Steak | *Steak* 20

La Régalade | *French* 26

Ocean Club | *Pac. NW* 22

Salmon House | *Pac. NW* 21

YALETOWN

Amarcord | *Italian* 22

Z Blue Water Cafe | *Seafood* 26

Brix | *Pac. NW* 21

Z Cioppino's | *Med.* 28

Elixir Bistro | *French* 23

glowbal grill | *Eclectic* 21

Goldfish | *Pac. NW* 20

Z Keg Steak | *Steak* 20

La Terrazza | *Italian* 25

Provence Marina | *French* 23

Rodney's Oyster | *Seafood* 24

NEW r.tl | *Eclectic* 25

Simply Thai | *Thai* 23

Victoria & Vancouver Island

DOWNTOWN

NEW Aura | *Pac. NW* 24

NEW Bard/Banker Public Hse. | *Pub* 18

Blue Crab | *Seafood* 23

Blue Fox Cafe | *Eclectic* 22

Z Brasserie L'Ecole | *French* 27

Cafe Brio | *Pac. NW* 26

Camille's | *Pac. NW* 27

Z Empress Rm. | *Pac. NW* 23

Ferris' Oyster Bar | *Seafood* 22

Il Terrazzo | *Italian* 24

J & J Wonton | *Chinese* 24

Z Keg Steak | *Steak* 20

Lure | *Seafood* 24

Pagliacci's | *Italian* 21

Pescatore | *Pac. NW/Seafood* 20

NEW Pizzeria Prima | *Pizza* 21

Rebar | *Eclectic/Veg.* 25

Red Fish | *Seafood* 25

Rest. Matisse | *French* 26

Siam Thai | *Thai* 21

Stage | *Med.* 26

Temple | *Pac. NW* 21

Zambri's | *Italian* 26

LANGFORD

Z Panache | *Pac. NW* 28

Smoken Bones | *BBQ/Creole* 23

MALAHAT

Aerie Resort | *French/Pac. NW* 25

OAK BAY

Marina | *Pac. NW/Seafood* 21

Paprika Bistro | *French/Italian* 27

SAANICH

Z Keg Steak | *Steak* 20

SALT SPRING ISLAND

Z Hastings Hse. | *Pac. NW* 27

SHAWNIGAN LAKE

Amusé Bistro | *French* 23

SIDNEY

Deep Cove | *French* 26

Haro's | *Pac. NW* 20

SOOKE

NEW Edge | *Pac. NW* -

Z Sooke Harbour | *Pac. NW* 27

TOFINO

Pointe/Wickaninnish | *Pac. NW* 25

Z Sobo | *Eclectic* 27

Whistler

Z Araxi | *Pac. NW* 26

Aubergine Grille | *Pac. NW* 24

Z Bear Foot Bistro | *Pac. NW* 27

Caramba! | *Med.* 18

Z Edgewater Lodge | 23
   Continental/Pac. NW

Elements | *Eclectic* 25

Fifty Two 80 | *Pac. NW* 22

Z Hy's Steak | *Steak* 23

Il Caminetto | *Italian* 24

Z Keg Steak | *Steak* 20

Z La Rua | *Pac. NW* 25

Monk's Grill | *Eclectic* 18

Mountain Club | *Pac. NW* 21

Quattro/Whistler | *Italian* 23

Z Rim Rock | *Pac. NW/Seafood* 26

Splitz Grill | *Burgers* 19

Sushi Village | *Japanese* 23

Tratt. di Umberto | *Italian* 24

Wildflower | *Pac. NW* 22

Nightlife Locations

Includes venue names and Appeal ratings.

Vancouver

DOWNTOWN

AuBAR Nightclub	18
☑ Bacchus Lounge	26
Ceili's Irish Pub	-
Cellar Nightclub	18
☑ Commodore Ballrm. *1929*	26
Ginger Sixty Two	21
900 West Lounge	20
Odyssey *GAY*	17
Railway Club	24
Shark Club	20
Yale Hotel	20

EAST SIDE

Cascade Room	-

LANGLEY

Shark Club	20

WEST END

Celebrities *GAY*	21

WEST SIDE

Rossini's	-

YALETOWN

Bar None	21
George Ultra Lounge	-
☑ Opus Bar *bathway TV*	23

Victoria & Vancouver Island

DOWNTOWN

Bengal Lounge	28
Shark Club	20
Sticky Wicket Pub	22

Whistler

Dubh Linn Gate	23
Garibaldi Lift B&G	23
Longhorn Saloon	20
Savage Beagle	-

Hotel Locations

Includes hotel names and Room ratings.

Vancouver

DOWNTOWN

Fairmont	21
Fairmont Waterfront	25
Four Seasons	23
NEW Loden Vancouver	-
Pacific Palisades	20
Pan Pacific	25
NEW Shangri-La Vancouver	-
Sutton Place	24
Wedgewood	24
Westin Bayshore	23
Westin Grand	24

RICHMOND

Fairmont Vancouver Air.	27

YALETOWN

Opus	24

Victoria & Vancouver Island

MALAHAT

Aerie	25

SALT SPRING ISLAND

Hastings House	24

SOOKE

Sooke Harbour	25

TOFINO

Wickaninnish Inn	27

VICTORIA

Fairmont Empress	21
Grand Pacific	24
Westin Bear Mtn.	-

Whistler

Adara	-
Fairmont/Whistler	24
Four Seasons	28
Pan Pacific	26
Westin	24